Can you hear the city whispering?

Maegan Broadhurst and Immony Men

This project was created during the summer of 2010, during a two-month period of living in the city of Winnipeg. Originally, it was planned to continue projects that we started in Montreal during our stay. However, while working in our makeshift studio in our apartment, the sounds of the city seemed to hijack our thought process and invite us into a completely new realm of exploration. This consistent beckoning from the city, brought about "Can you hear the city whispering?".

First and foremost we would like to thank the participants who took time to contribute to our project. Without you this collaboration between us and the city would not have been possible. Thank you for sharing your secret spots, memories, insights, and fondness for your city with us.

Thank you to Mary Reid and Kerri-Lynn Reeves for giving us the opportunity to bring the project back to the community, at the "My city's still breathing" symposium. Thank you for your enthusiasm and support throughout the process.

Thank you to hannh_g for giving us the opportunity to take part in her Tallest Poppy artist residency. The experience allowed us to connect further with the locals, as they graciously provided written statements and engaged in insightful dialogue. Thank you to the Tallest Poppy for feeding us their wonderful Sunday brunch.

Thank you to Aceartinc for giving the project a space to share the explored locations, and the opportunity to introduce our book to Winnipeg.

Thank you to our friends and co-workers for helping us understand what your city is about, showing us around, and being so welcoming and kind hearted.

Thank you Winnipeg.

Table of Contents

Section One

Process

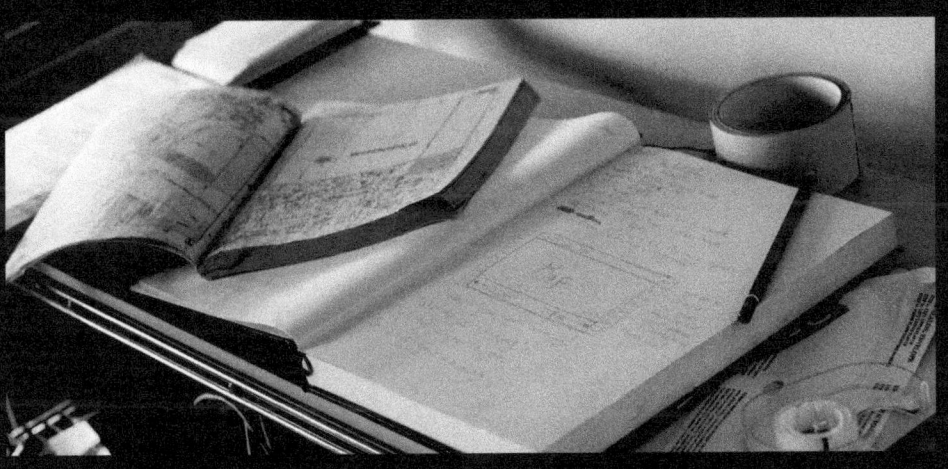

Discovering the city

Can you hear the city whispering? Started during the summer months of 2010. The two of us decided to move here for the summer, for a summer job. Neither of us had never been to Winnipeg before this trip. Our original plan was to continue work that we had previously started in Montreal. However, Winnipeg was much too intriguing not the enter our work. We spent hours working in our makeshift studio, where sounds of the city trickled through the windows. It wasn't before long that we decided to create a project that focused on the city as it's key component.

Stepping outside into the city was a much different experience than we had expected. Montreal being our hometown, we thought we were pretty adept at navigating a city space. It was a bit of a shock to find out that our apartment looks out onto a rougher area of the city. These areas did not only look desolate, but they seem to be dangerous. Each night we heard loud sirens and people from the park across from us. It just seems like the area and the people in it are in a constant state of distress. We made some friends who are born and raised in Winnipeg. One of our first questions was: "Which areas are safe to walk around in the city?"

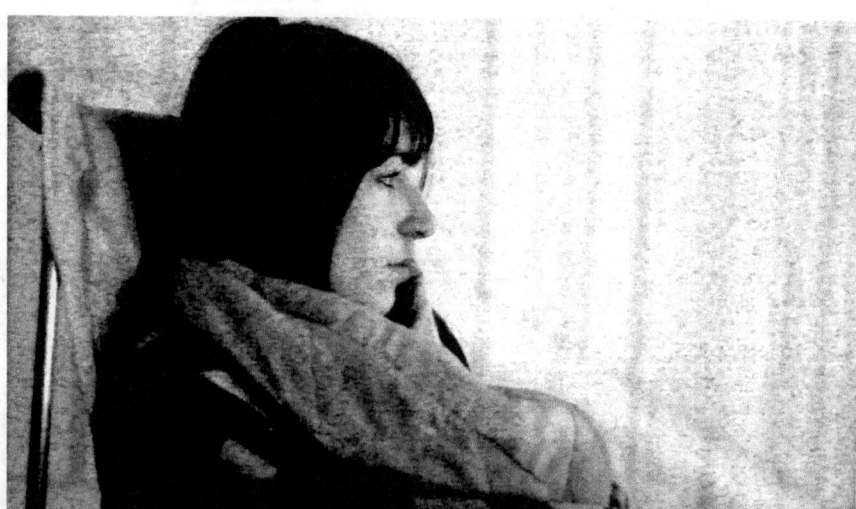

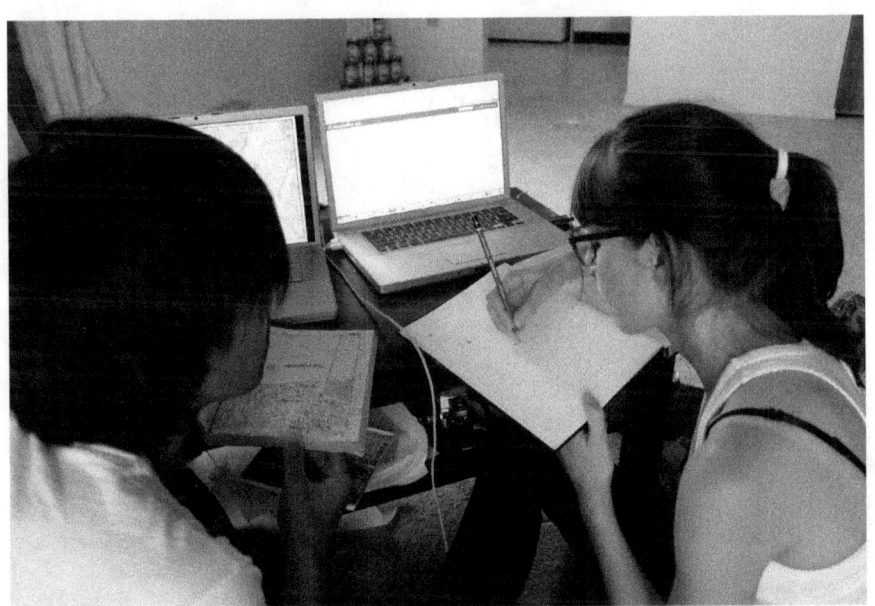

Inviting the Public
Tourist like approach

Back in Montreal and Windsor, we've documented sites through video and photography. Having lived in these cities we understood the history and context of those sites. In Winnipeg we found ourselves combing the city documenting sites whose origins were completely alien to us.

We found ourselves frequently asking, "What is actually happening here?" We realized that we were looking at these sites through an outsider's perspective, and what we need is some insight from people who reside within the city. Much like our first week when we asked our local friends about the area, we needed to approach the project with a tourist's perspective in order to get the right set of questions.

Inviting the Public
How/Why?

We began to devise our approach to invite locals as collaborators into our project. We wanted a simple, accessible, commitment-free, way to address the public with our questions. We decided that the best way to invite locals to interact with a map of their city, was through a flyer format. This way anyone could approach the flyer on their own account and present their information. It was a simple way that asked the participant to engage with our work in the present, and did not require them to visit a website, email us, or take any time out of their schedule to answer.

We gave them simple instructions; "Tell us what you think! Place a sticker on your favorite spot and one on a place you dislike. Thank you." We also added colored stickers to make it clear which spots were favorites and which ones were disliked. Labeling them "I Like" (with green and yellow stickers) or "I Don't" (with red and blue stickers).

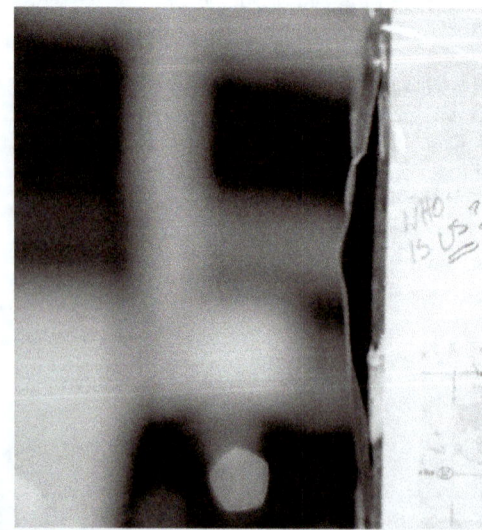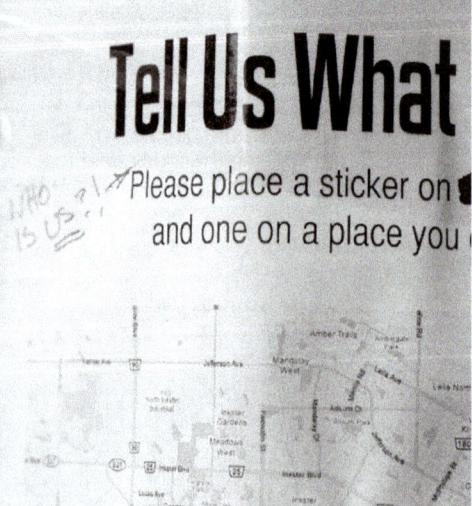

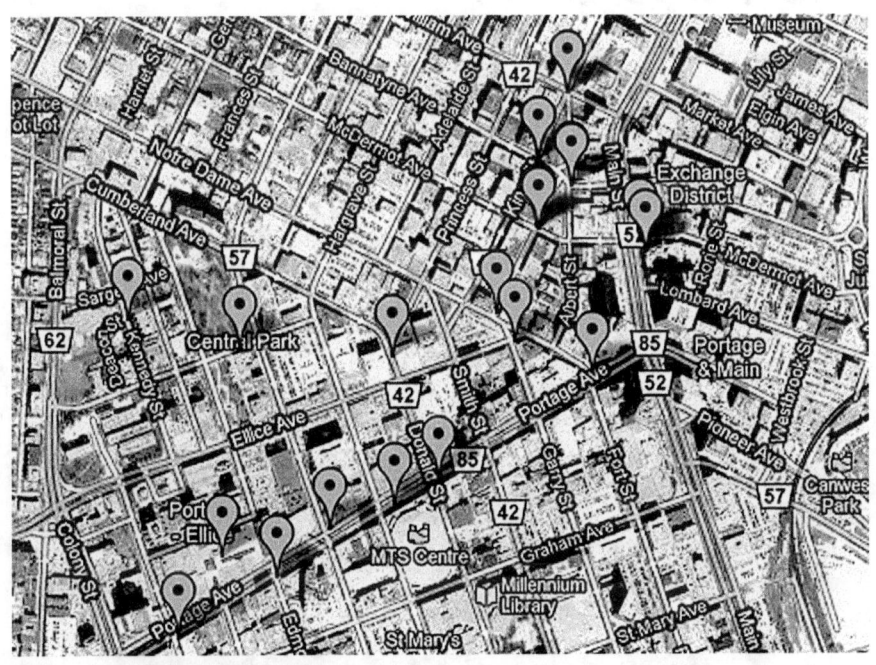

Inviting the Public
Where?

The first round of flyer installation we used as a test to see if this format would culti-
vate interaction. We posted 25 flyers around the Exchange District, Main Street, and
Portage Avenue. We focused on placing flyers at bus terminals, ensuring not only pedestrians living in the city core participated, it granted commuters who live in the
suburb a chance to tell us what they thought.

Flyer Response

Our test run was successful, so we posters up 25 more flyers, this time around the Osborne area. We made the decision to leave the posters up, and let the city and elements wipe them away. Our strategy was to photograph each poster consecutively for a week. Some posters were removed before the end of this time, but because of our approach we still had the data in our photographic database. The two-week period of continual documentation of the flyers resulted in 445 liked and disliked areas chosen by individuals who reside in Winnipeg.

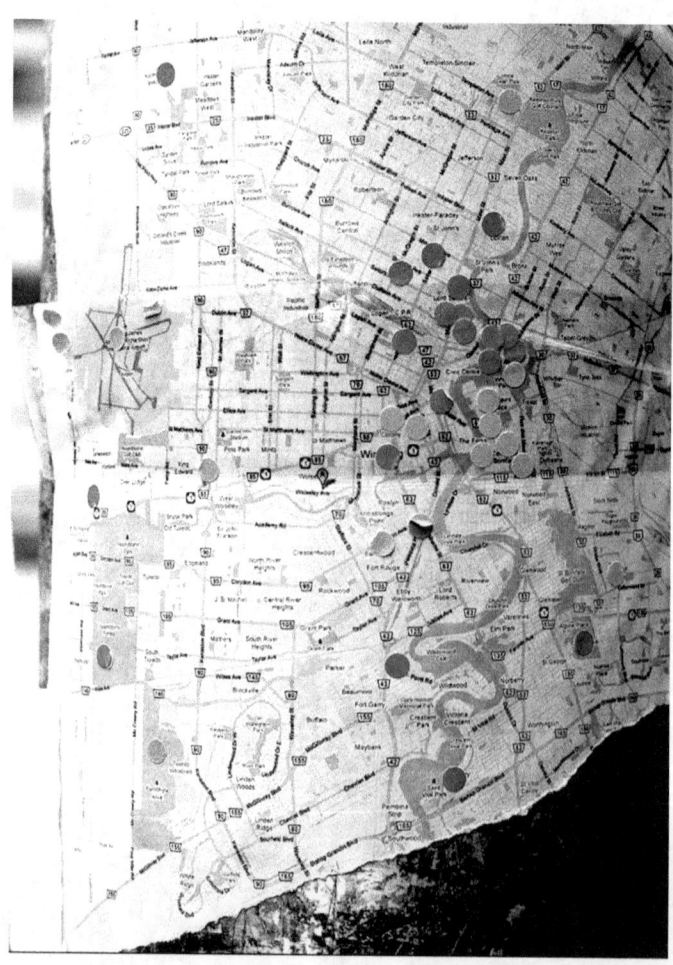

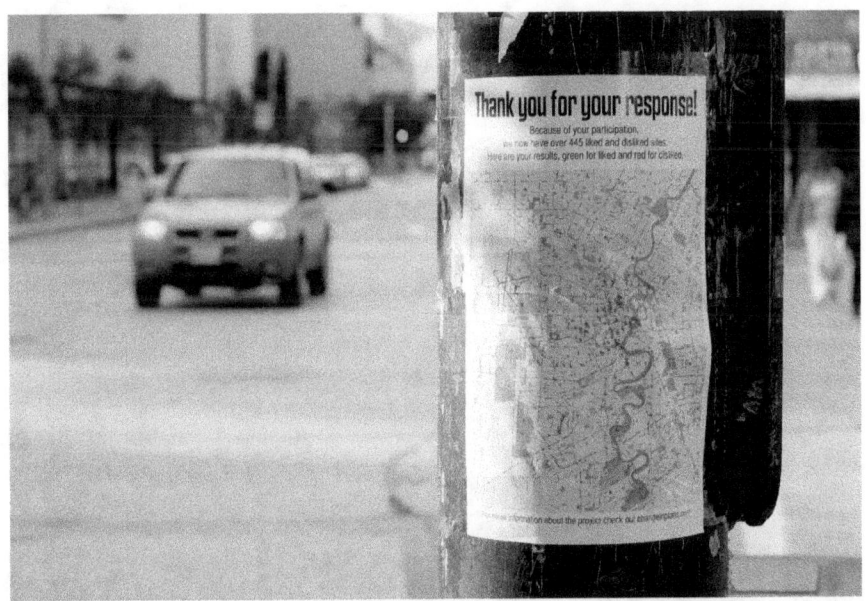

"Give back" Flyer

As a gesture of appreciation, we decided to post a final round of posters up in the same location of the originals. The new poster was again a map of Winnipeg, but this time all 445 sites were visible. Letting the public know what sites they have chosen as a community.

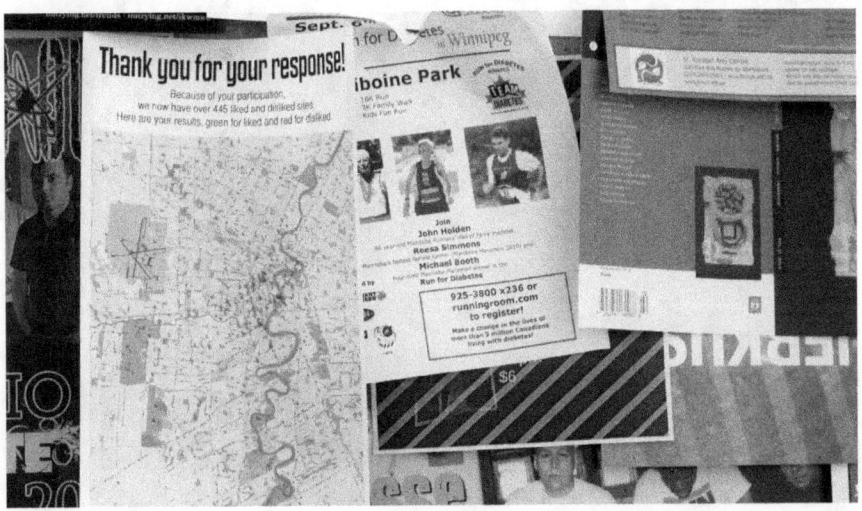

Flyer Documentation

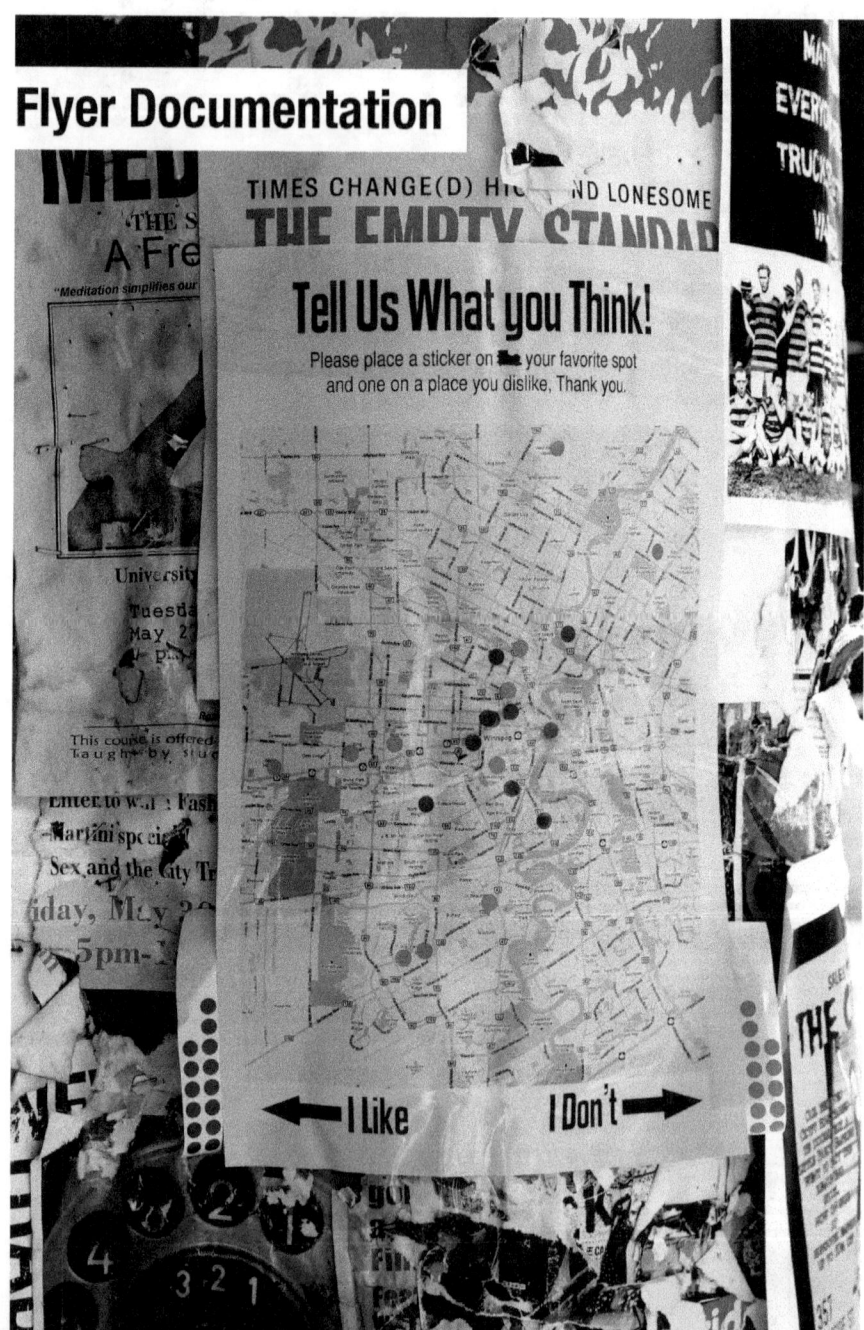

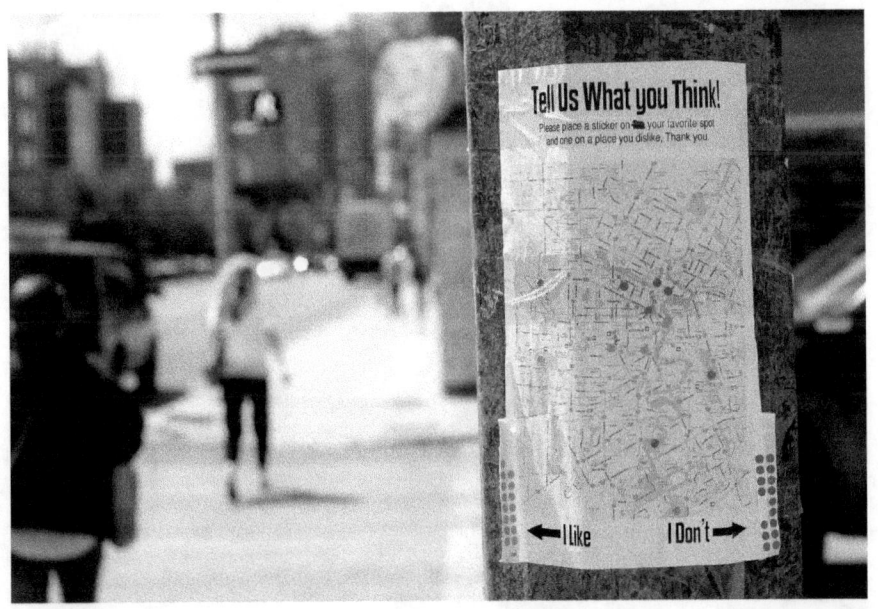

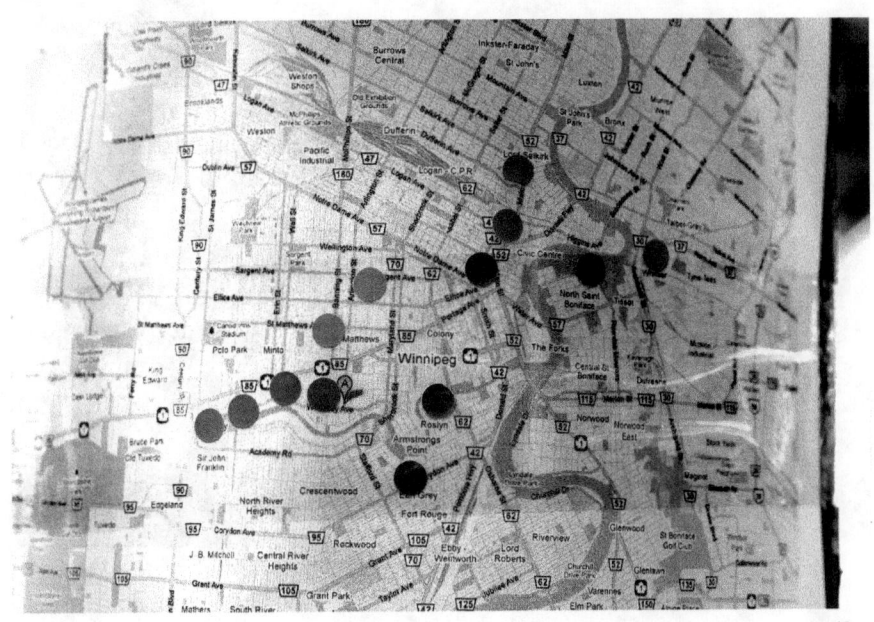

Tangible Database
Large Apartment Map

Our first attempt at creating a database, was in the form of a six-foot by six-foot map that covered our apartment wall. Creating a tangible database allowed us to cluster sites and create a plan of action. Before conducting fieldwork, we'd outline an area for research and print out a smaller more detailed map of the area.

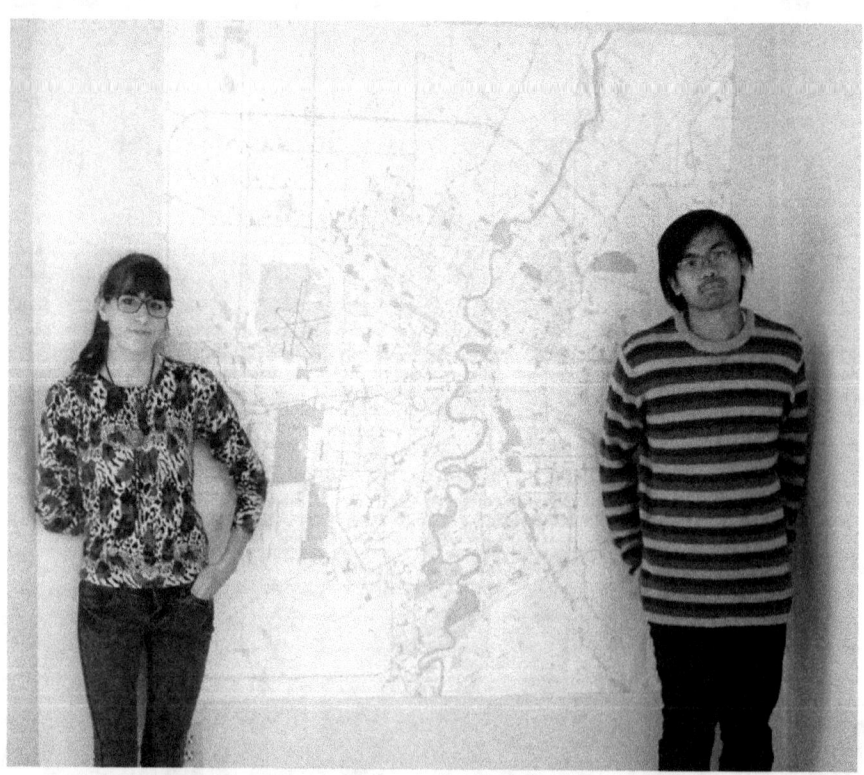

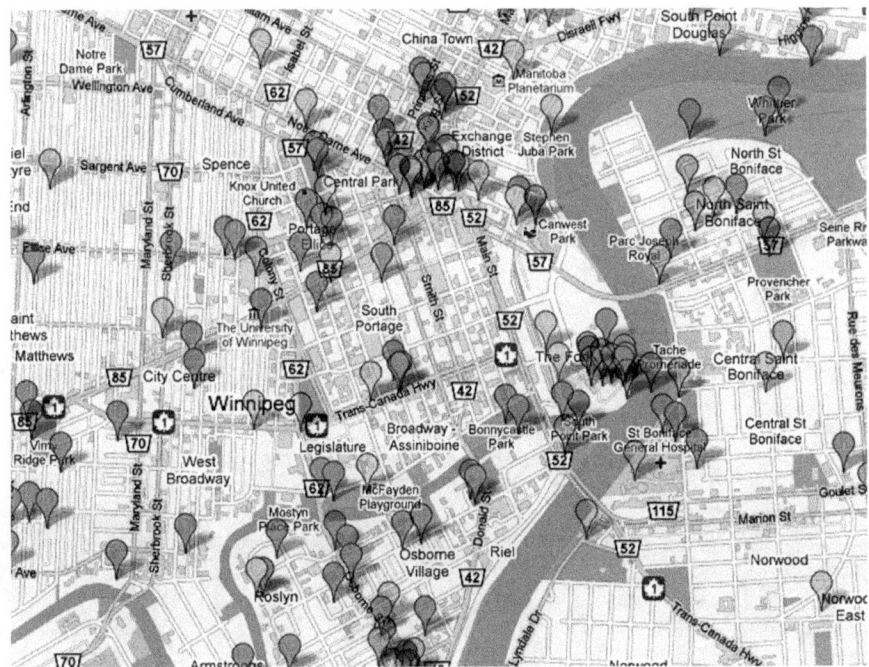

Clustering

This map also made clustering of liked and disliked areas more visible. Clusters of red and green dots pinning down common areas of interest such as the international airport, the civic centre, and the forks. There are strong emotions placed towards parks and they are either liked or disliked.

Google Maps Database

In addition to our large map we've decided to create a database for the spots and use Google Earth as a platform for mapping out the locations.

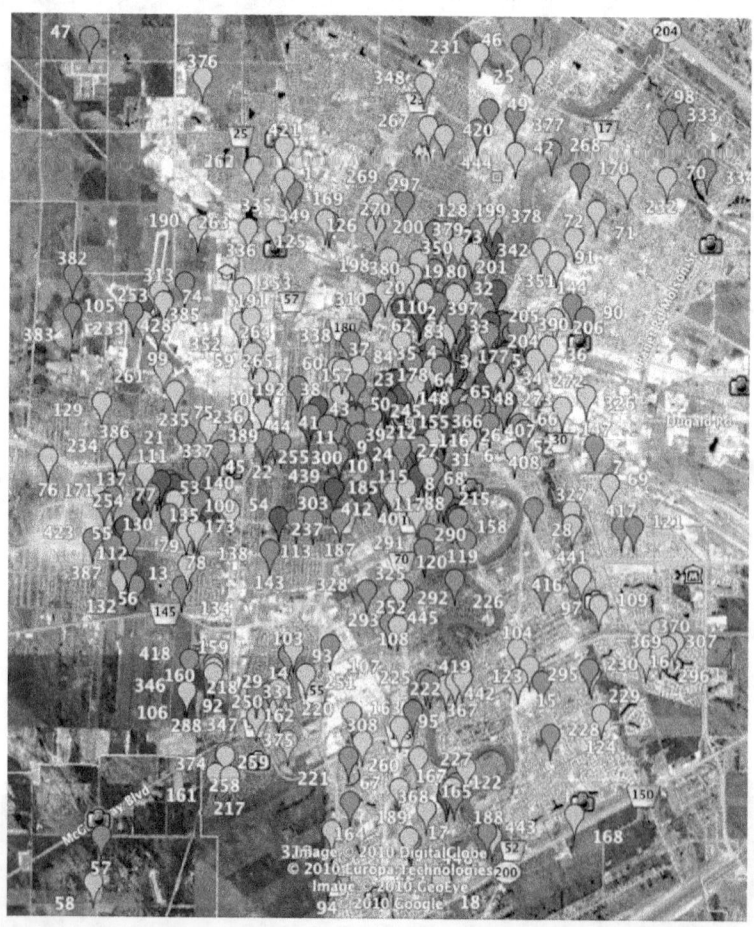

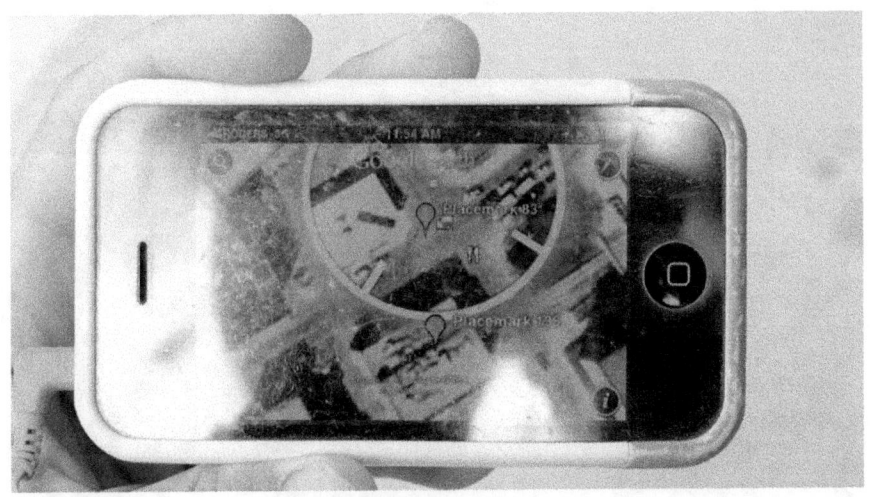

Using the Database during fieldwork

Having the google map database as a portable reference during fieldwork was an irreplaceable tool for this stage. Having the database available on our iPhone allowed us to reference the data in an interactive way. The database would create a marker notifying us where we were in relation to a site. The map also had the capability of zooming in or zooming out, letting us see specific street names the site was located on. Google street could also be used giving us a virtual path instructing us on our route.

Field Research: Part 1
Our Approach

The next process was documenting the selected sites. In early field research stages, we travelled on foot from site-to-site. This was more exhausting then productive. In order to cover ground we needed a faster way. This resulted in the two of us renting bikes from the Hi hostel which was a block away from our apartment. With bicycles, larger distances could be covered in a day. Separating the database into north-east, south-west type clusters we could systematically plan our routes beforehand.

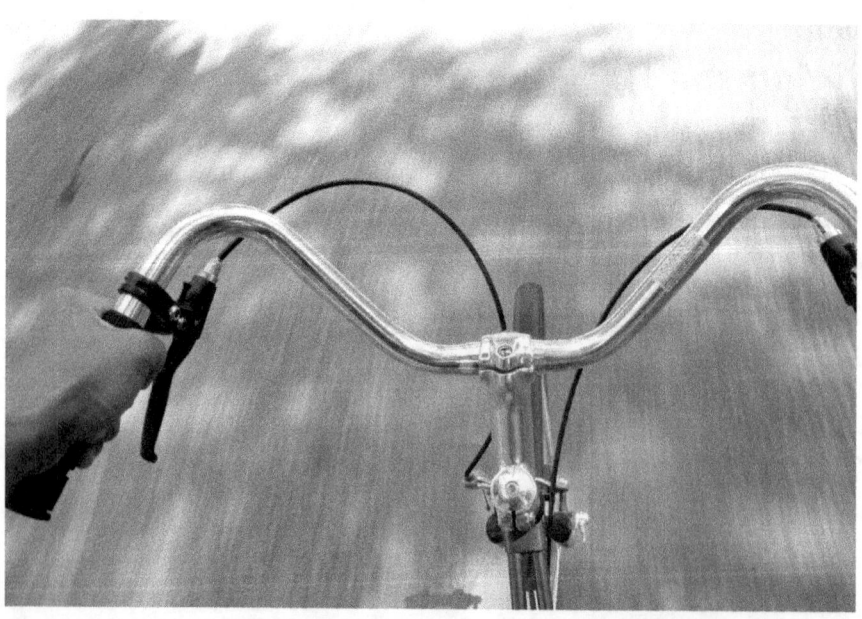

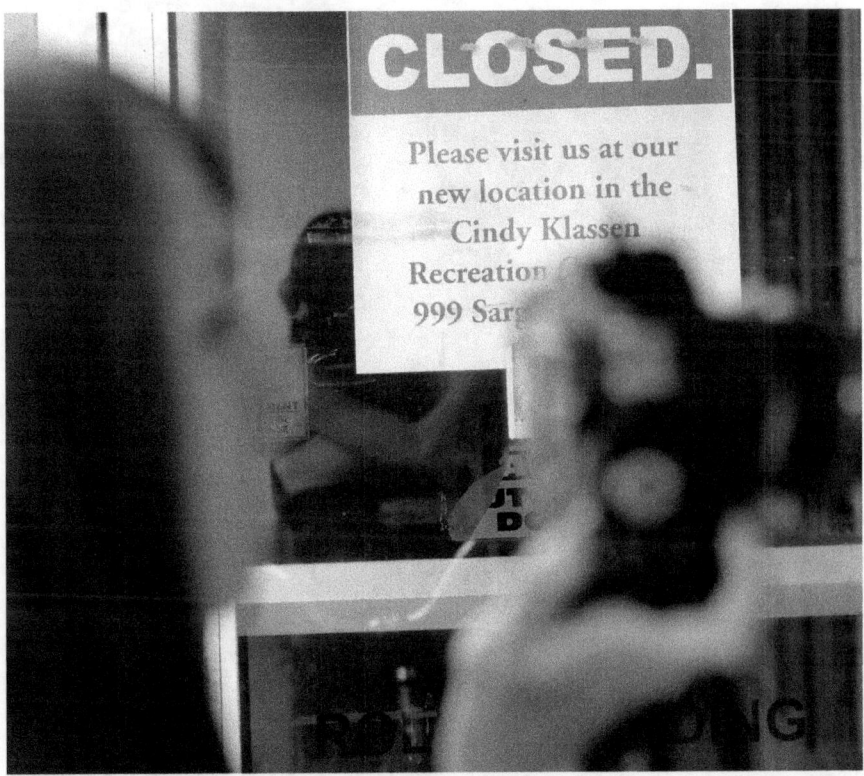

How easy was it to find the "site"

At first we weren't too sure how accurate the markers were and what we were looking for besides street names and identifiable buildings/establishments. We combed
up and down the city following our map and after our first day we discovered it was
quite easy to notice the negative or positive attributes of each site.

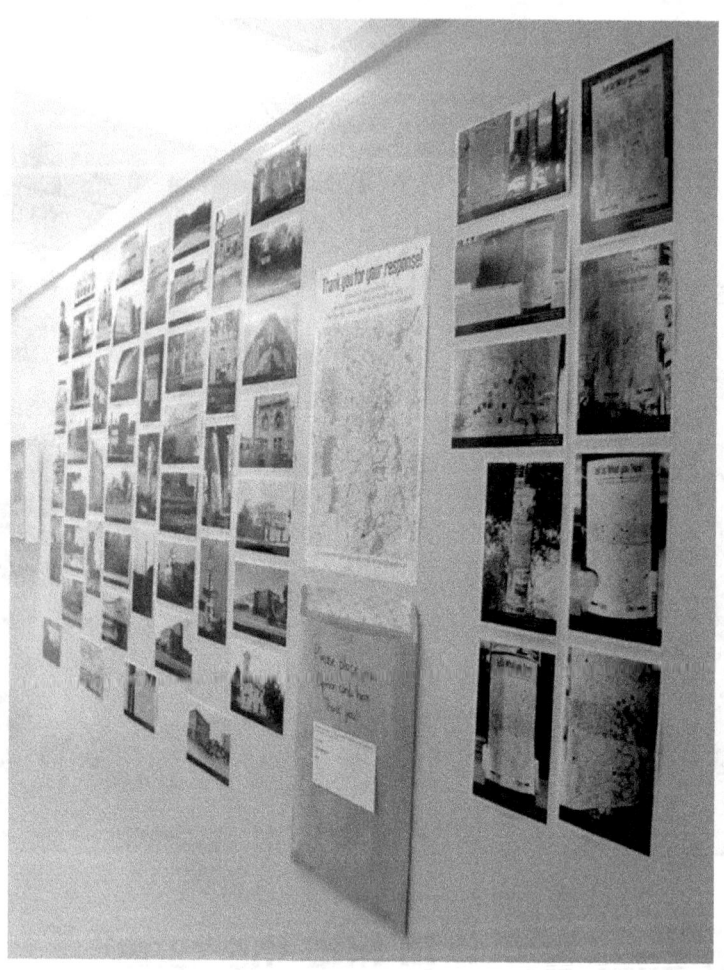

Field Research: Part 2
Tallest poppy residency

After compiling our site documentation, we wanted to inquire more feedback about the sites we visited from people who were willing to talk about them. After meeting hannah_g from aceartinc. She gave us an opportunity to do just that. Taking part in her Tallest Poppy artist residency for a day, allowed us to present our documentation to a local audience. After displaying the photographs on the wall of the restaurant, we gave each customer an opinion card to fill out about a location up on the wall.

Gathering Information
Local's Explanations and Feelings of the sites

The customers were graciously receptive to our project, all responded to a location. Some engaged in conversation with us, and we discussed Winnipeg as a city in general. These dialogues were so insightful in understanding the city, it's attitude, and the people that make the area. We came to a conclusion that day. That Winnipeg was a cultural city, with a small town state of mind, community came first. The arts are thriving as a result of a tight-knit community, open to sharing and giving each other opportunities. Scattered around the city structure rests hints of the community giving heart, at times it's subtle, but even in the most impoverished areas it remains. We left the Tallest poppy that day with a handful of cue cards, with opinions, stories, and memories of people that made up these places we had been visiting for the past two and half months.

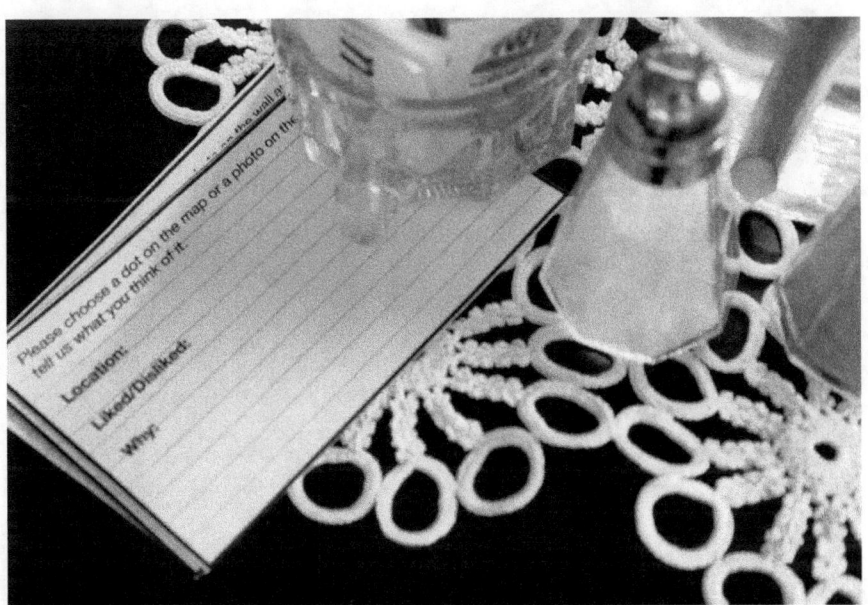

Research from a far

Leaving Winnipeg to return to Montreal our hometown, meant closing the chapter of our field research and opening a new phase of our project. At this point it was time to begin working on the final product, which was the travel guide. It is a strange thing writing about a city that you are so far away from. However, Winnipeg still seemed to be a very present element in our lives. It didn't seem as far away as we thought, and neither were the Winnipeg people. Something that came as a surprise to us, was the level of public interaction at a distance. During the book compilation, we frequently scoured the internet looking for clues about sites we had visited. During our internet research we would come in to contact with locals, who would enthusiastically share their experience with sites. These personal accounts via email were what the project needed to keep the product intimate.

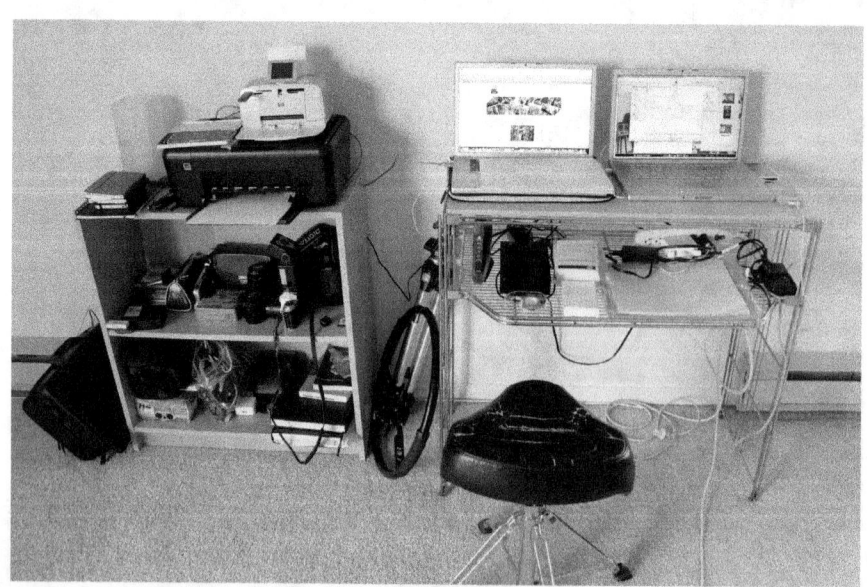

Section Two
Sites

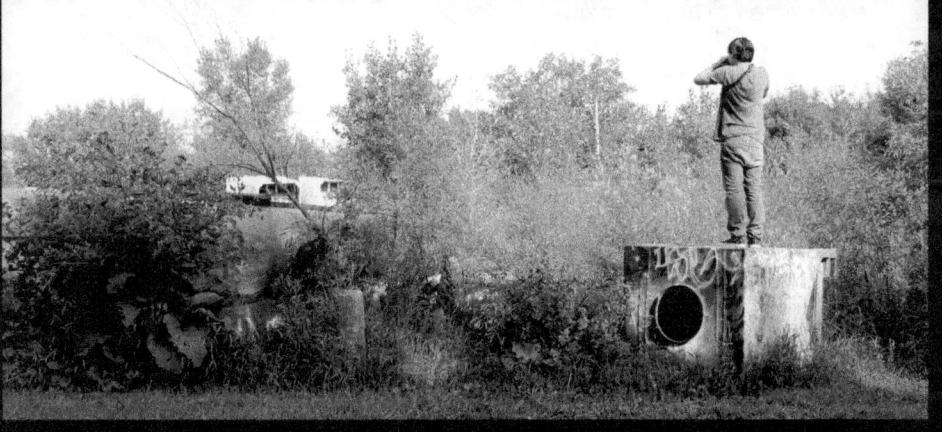

Chapter One
Traditional Landmarks

As expected we encountered a number of customary tourist sites. Among these are the forks, the golden boy, Cordyn Avenue, and St Boniface Cathedral. These locations attracted clusters of liked and the occasional disliked stickers. We anticipated this reaction to these specific sites, as tourists ourselves we had been told to visit such places well before our arrival in Winnipeg.

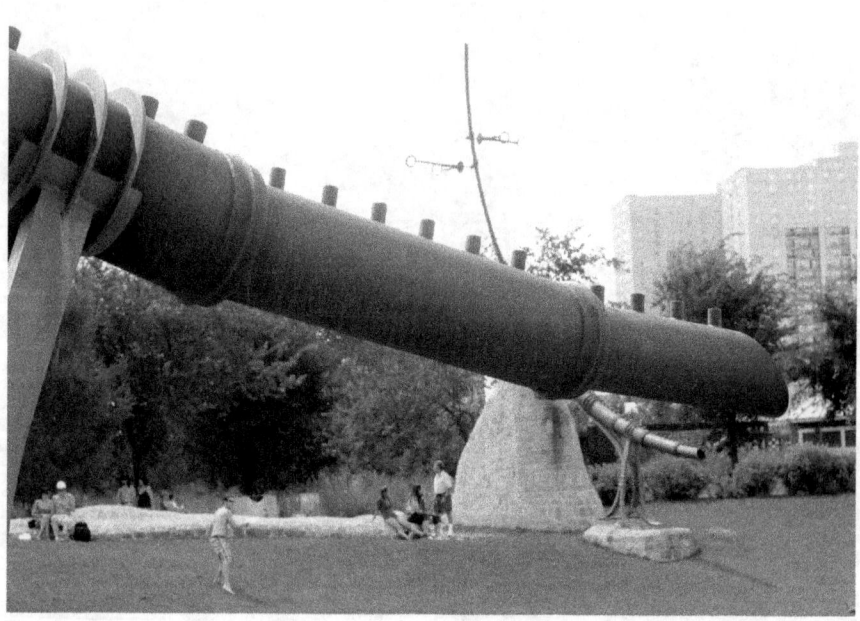

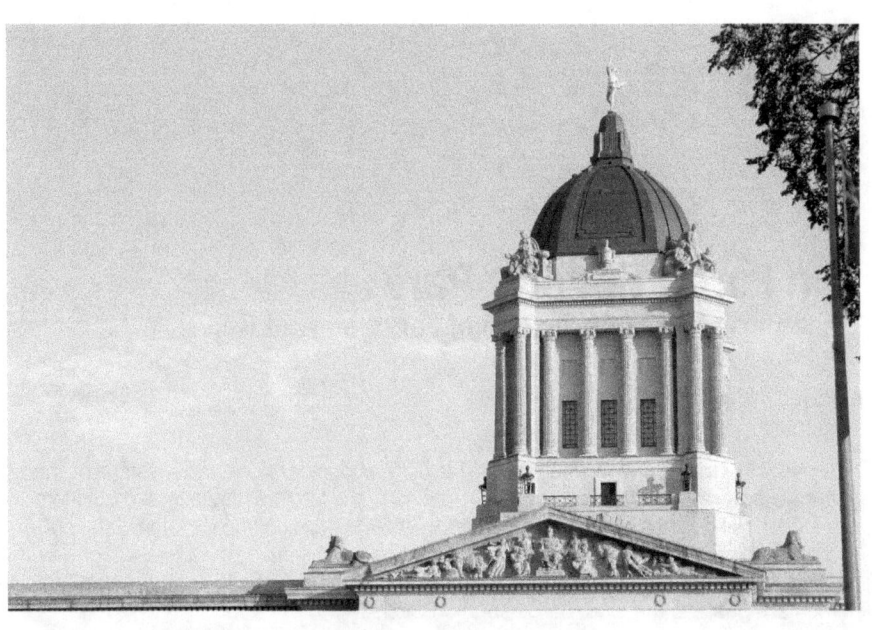

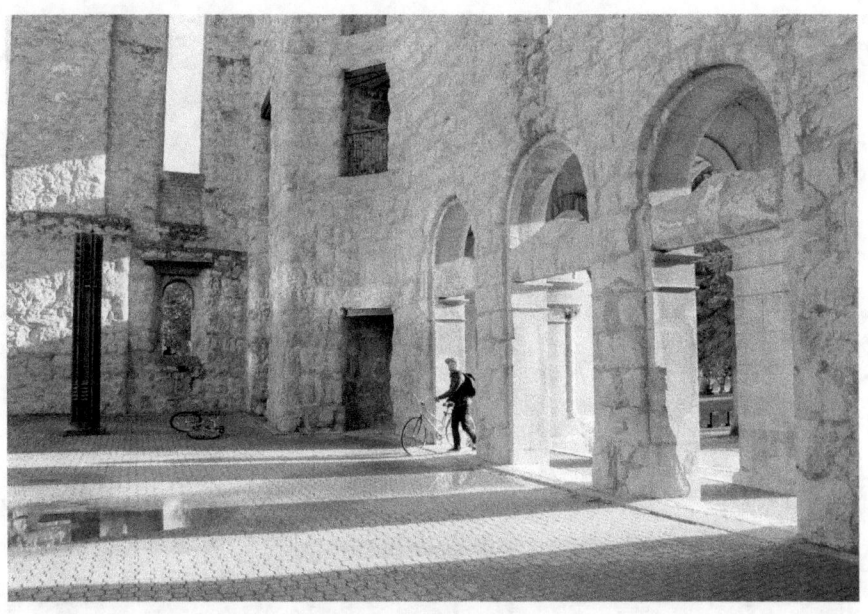

The Forks Historic Park
Placemarker 149: At the end of Forks Market Rd.

A spot for lazy weekend afternoons. Strolling alongside the muddy waters of the rivers. The gravel path crunches under your feet, the families of geese and duck are tail-up looking for brunch a foot away from walkway. You can hear motorboats, children running, wind blowing through branches and the hum of a distant highway. There are thoughts of the past scattered around the perimeter in the form of monuments, signs and the Oodena Celebration Circle.

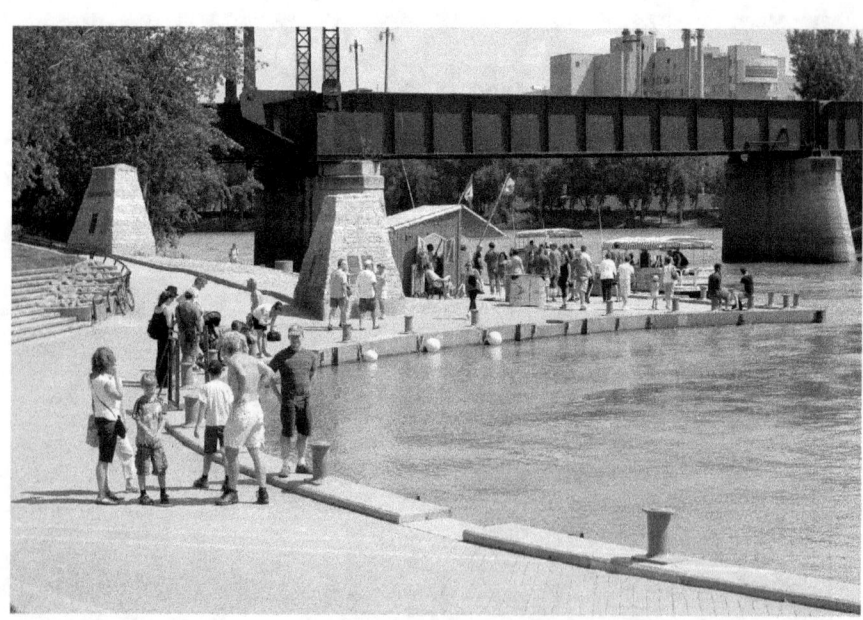

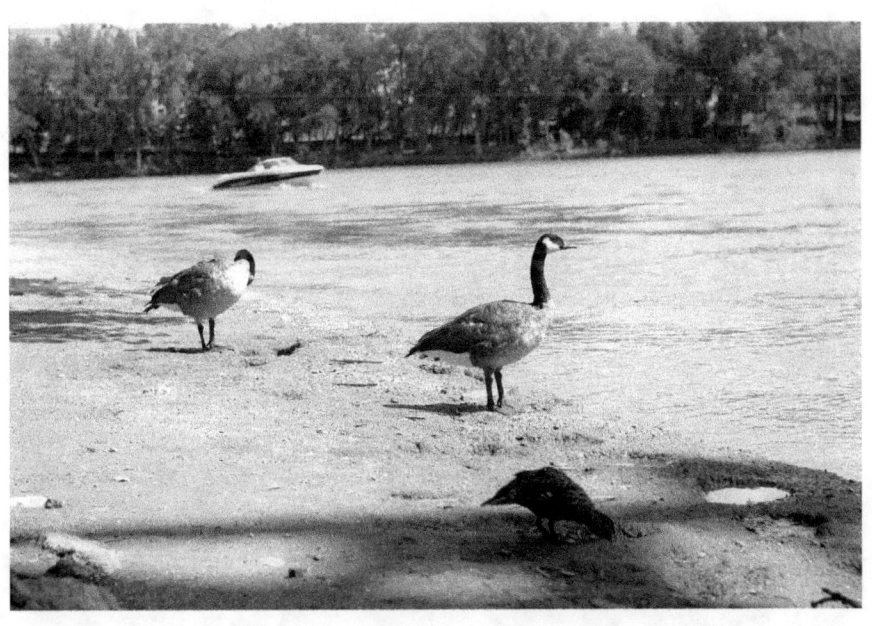

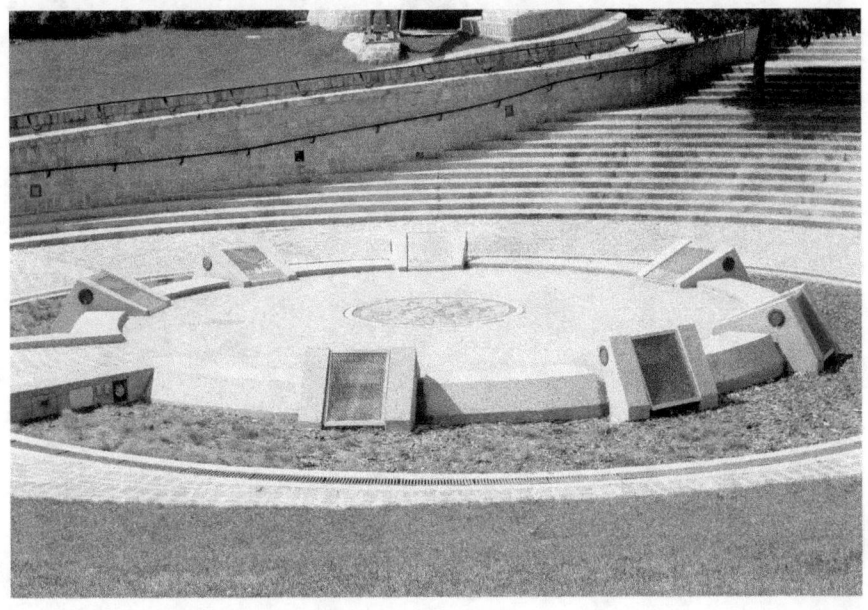

The Forks Walkway
Placemarker 246: Along the Red River's shore

"Peaceful, serene. One of the most beautiful locations for scenery in Winnipeg. Also, a very special place in my heart because that is where I went to my first date with the love of my life."

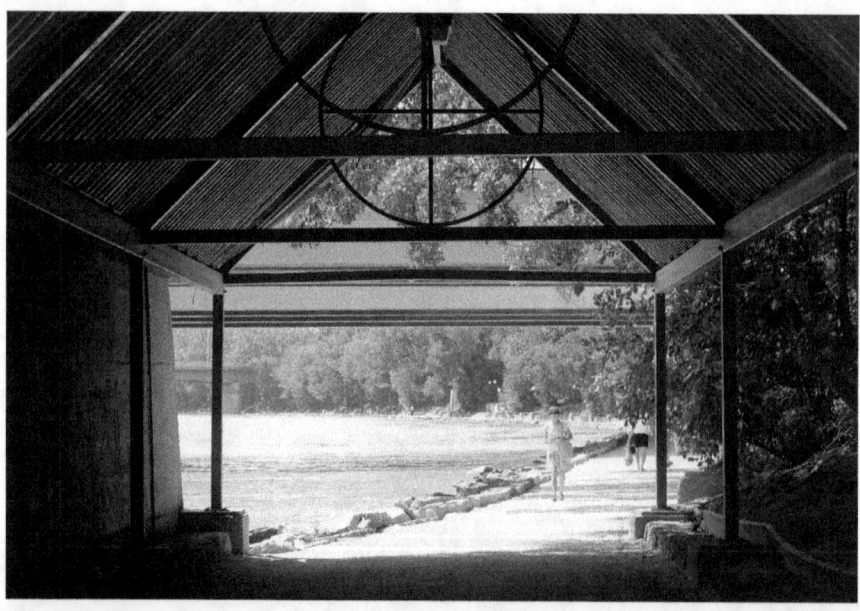

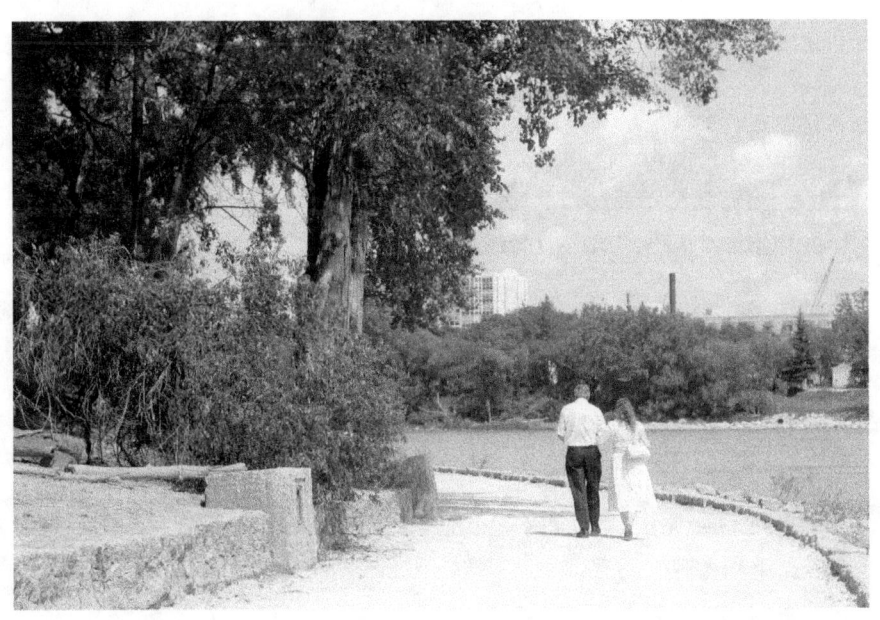

Please choose a dot on the map or a photo on the wall and tell us what you think of it.

Location: Forks walkway

Liked/Disliked: Liked

Why: Peaceful, serene. One of the most beautiful locations for scenery in Winnipeg. Also, a very special place in my heart because that is where I went for my first date with the love of my life.

The Forks Skate Plaza
Placemarker 179: Waterfront Drive and York Ave

The Forks skate plaza is one of Canada's first urban skate parks and is well known internationally for its unique design. "New line skate parks" has taken the plans of famous street skate spots from San Francisco, Barcelona, and Japan, condensing them into a 44,000 square feet concrete creation. The main section of the plaza contains various size stair sets, banks, and rails. Recreating these street spots in one given space is a real treat for skaters of all ages.

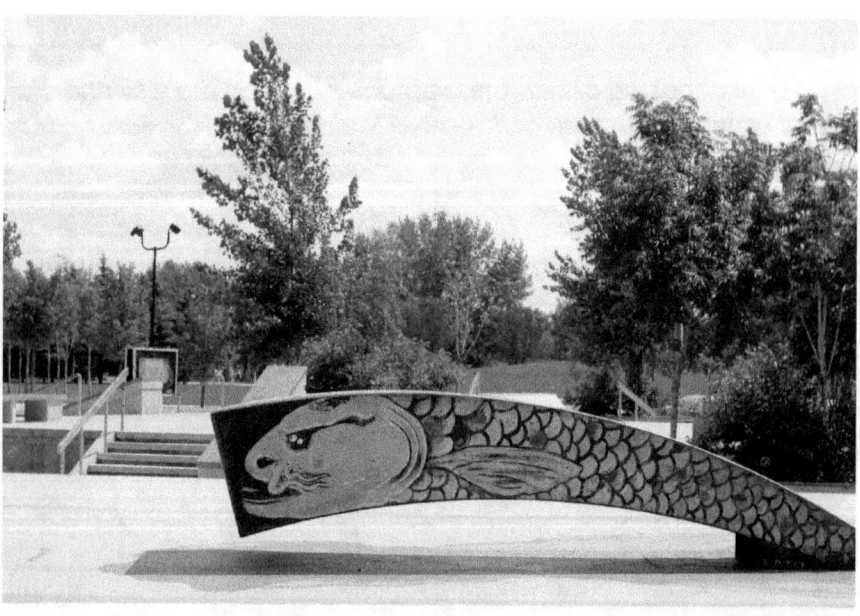

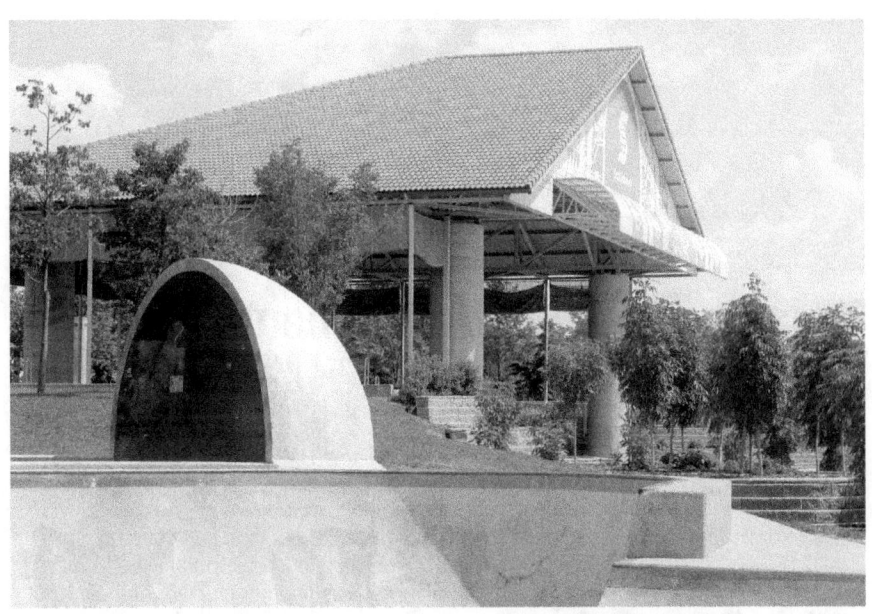

There are multiple ledges, bowls, and quarter pipes in all sorts of sizes and made from different types of materials. One can only be curious by the oddly shaped skate-able art sculptures and the height/ construction of the vert ramps. The skate patrol is a group of experience skateboarders who work at the park to greet newcomers and educated young skaters on etiquette in order to create an enjoyable atmosphere. This is a park located in the downtown core of Winnipeg and is a must for all skateboarders, in-line skaters, and BMX riders.

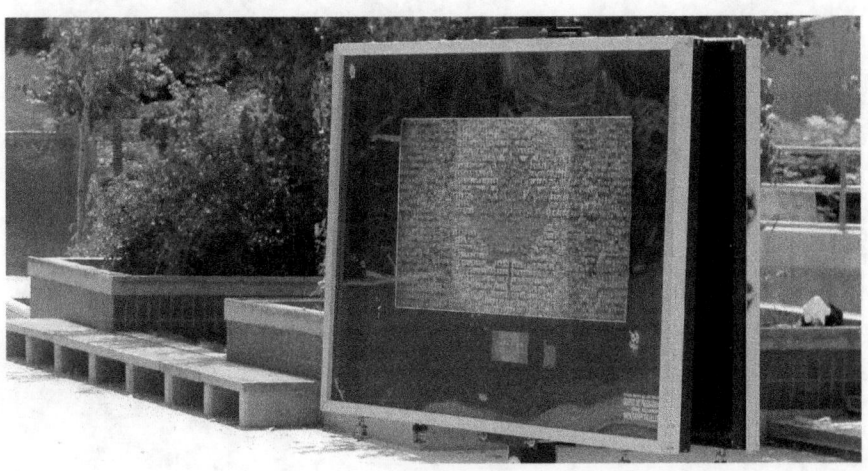

Canadian Museum for Human Rights
Placemarker 181: Main St. and Waterfront Dr.

Construction on the site is in full swing, and it hints of tomorrow's Winnipeg. The plans for the building's final appearance sits in front of the fenced off concrete shell as a promise. The site itself is in transition, the cranes have temporarily become a staple of Winnipeg's skyline. Soon to take it's place as another element of the city's pride: The Forks.

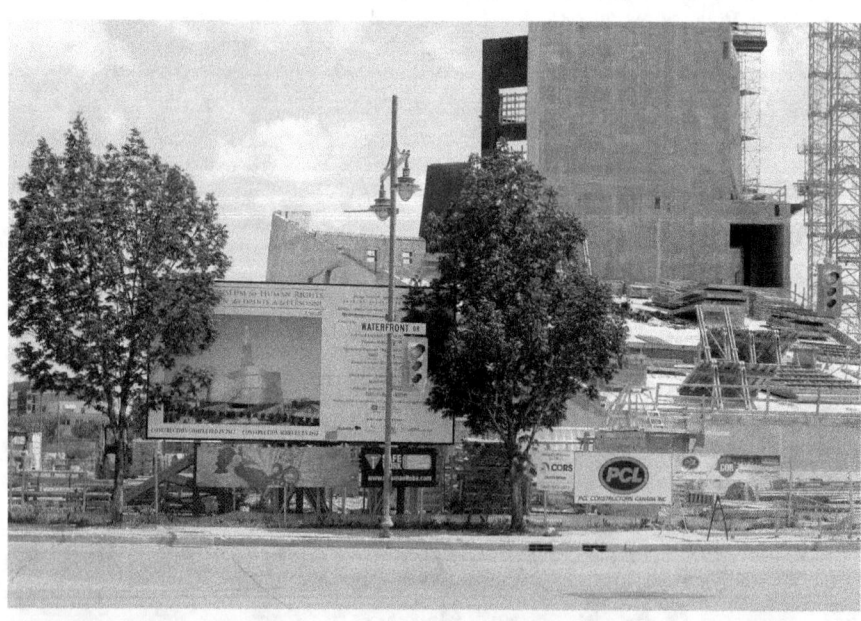

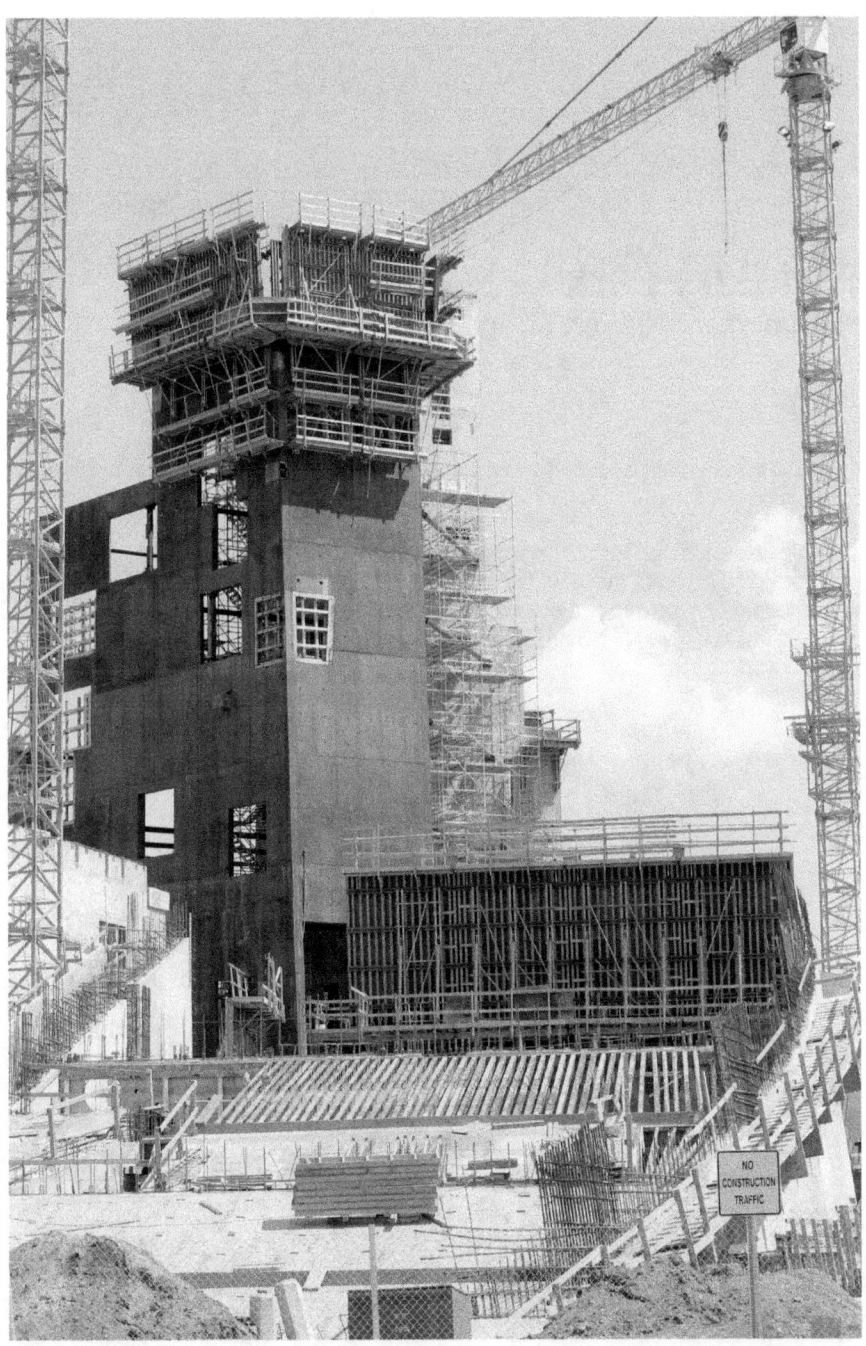

Fort Gary Park
Placemarker 319: Fort St. and Broadway

This site is an attempt at revitalizing a monument, in hopes to clutch on to Winnipeg's historical roots. The heart of an ancient structure remains, while faux attachments surround it, mimicking the fort walls. It is indeed "a somewhat pitiful marker for the oldest important building site in Winnipeg." (Thompson p. 63) Strategically placed plaques, with the site's history point to good intentions. However, they are weathered by time and rain and are no longer legible. Making the site's rich history a mystery to the visitor.

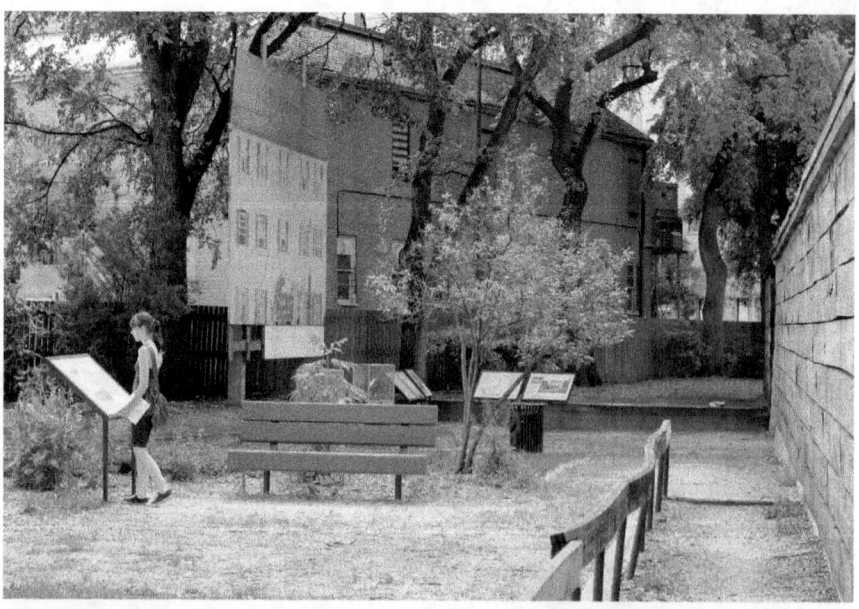

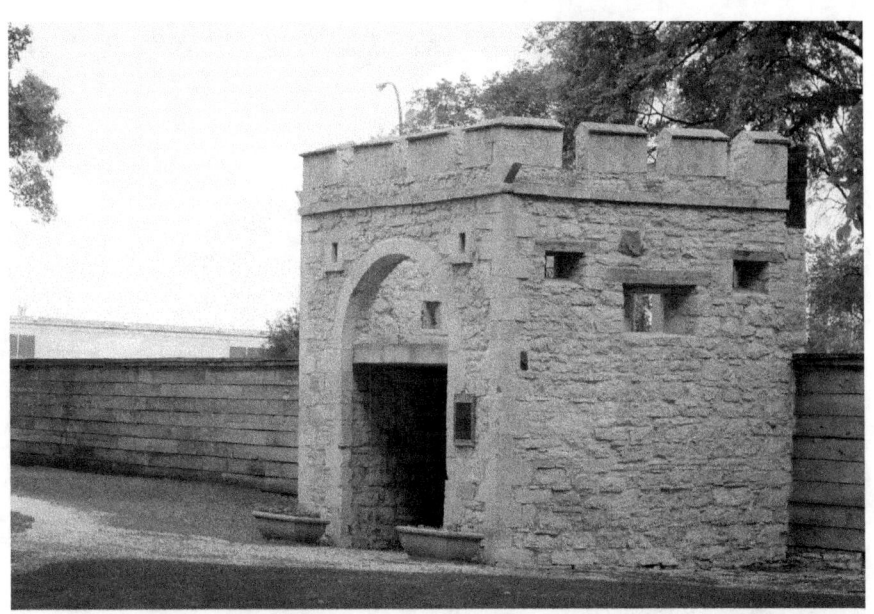

Broken beer bottles, lasagna and a McCain "Deep n' Delicious" cake are lying in the interior of the fort. Perhaps, this site is more than just a symbol of the past, maybe it is used as a late night clubhouse. Should we ask ourselves, what does Winnipeg's history mean to us? Does both the city and its inhabitants need to take more pride in the maintenance of Winnipeg's history? Can we do more? Should we do more?

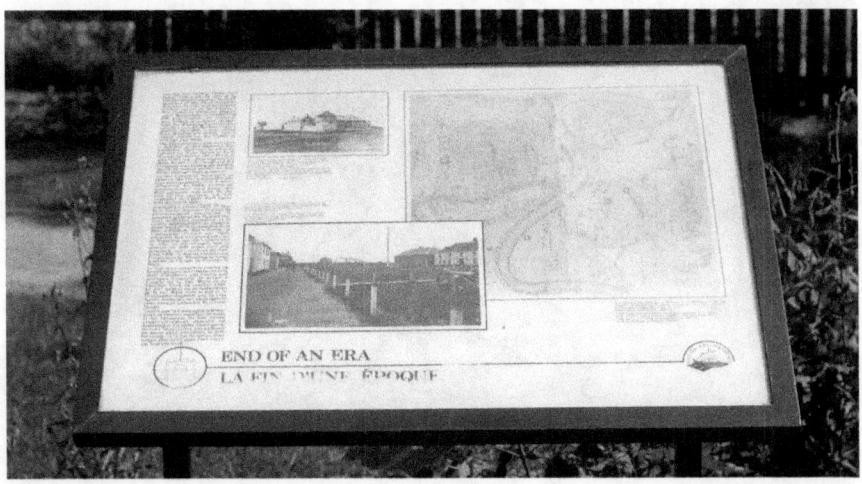

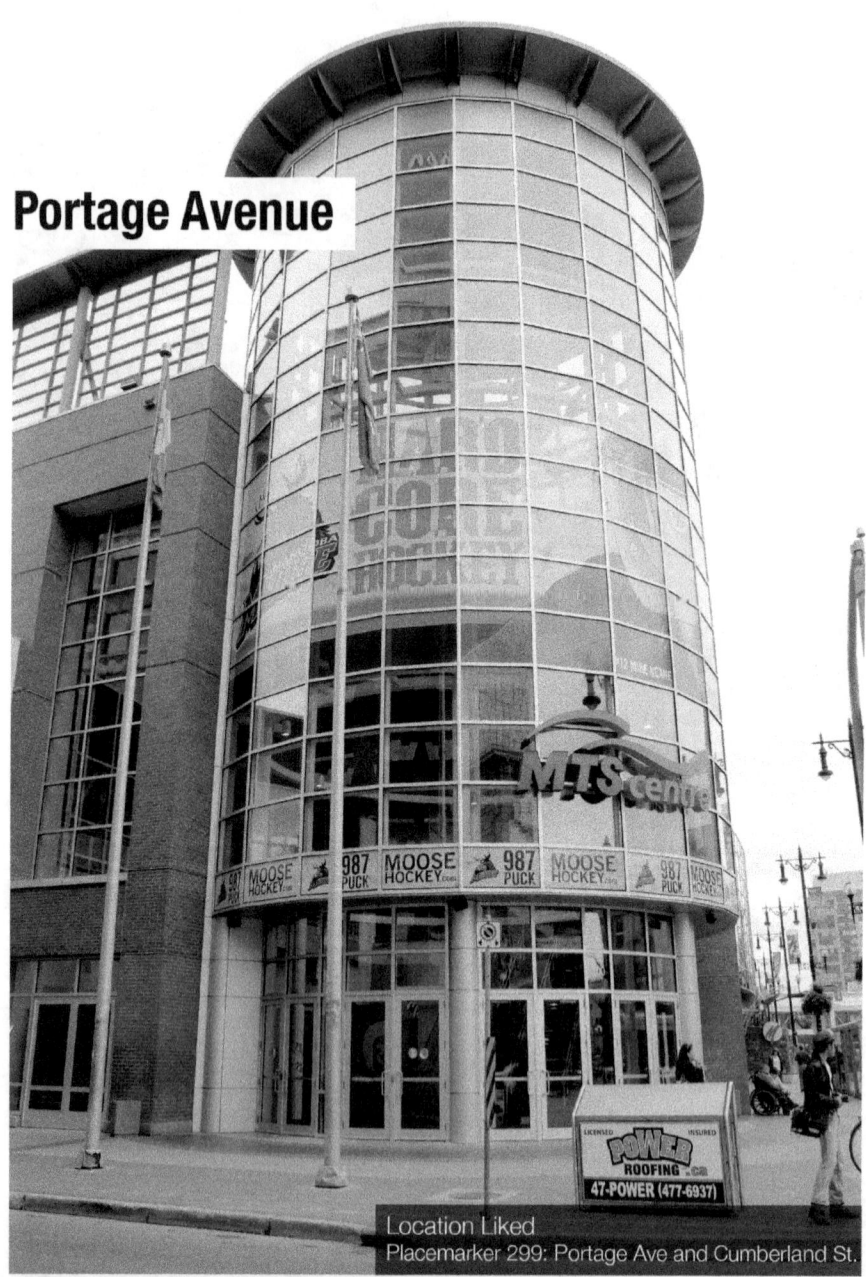

Portage Avenue

Location Liked
Placemarker 299: Portage Ave and Cumberland St.

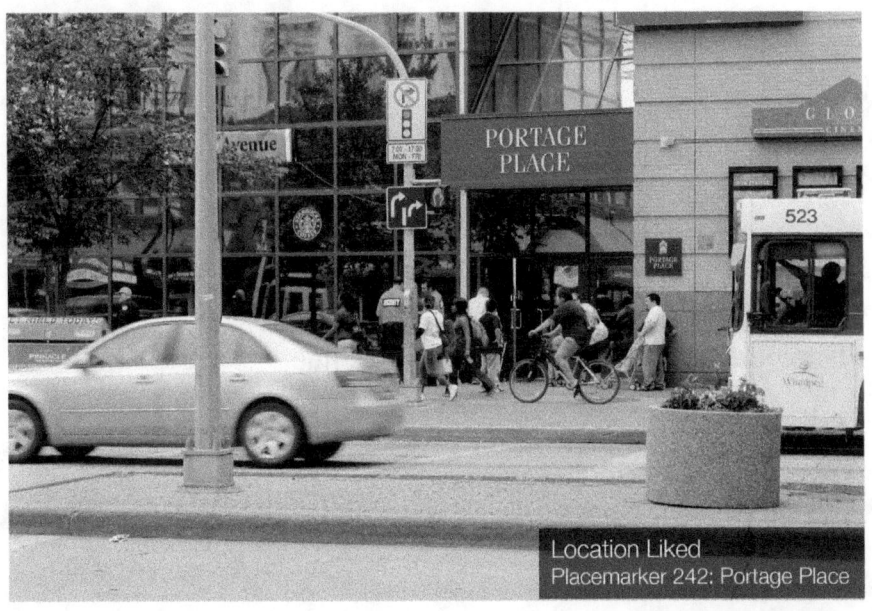

Location Liked
Placemarker 242: Portage Place

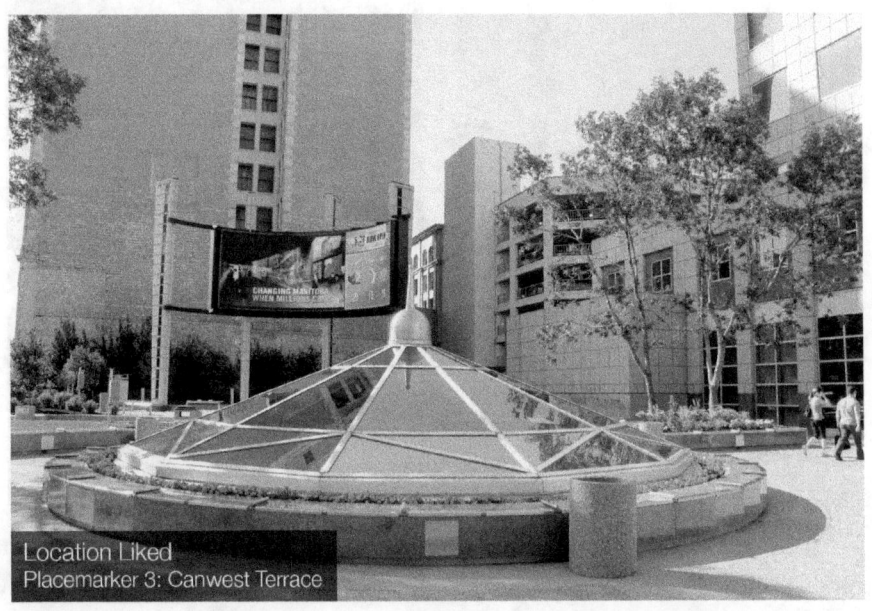

Location Liked
Placemarker 3: Canwest Terrace

Corydon Avenue
Placemarker 214/248/257: Corydon Avenue

At the edge of the Pembina highway, a cast iron arch introduces Corydon avenue with an air of old world grandeur. To tourists, the area is promoted as the "most eclectic character area of European diversity combined with Winnipeg hospitality." But to the local's it's a hub of activity during both day and night.

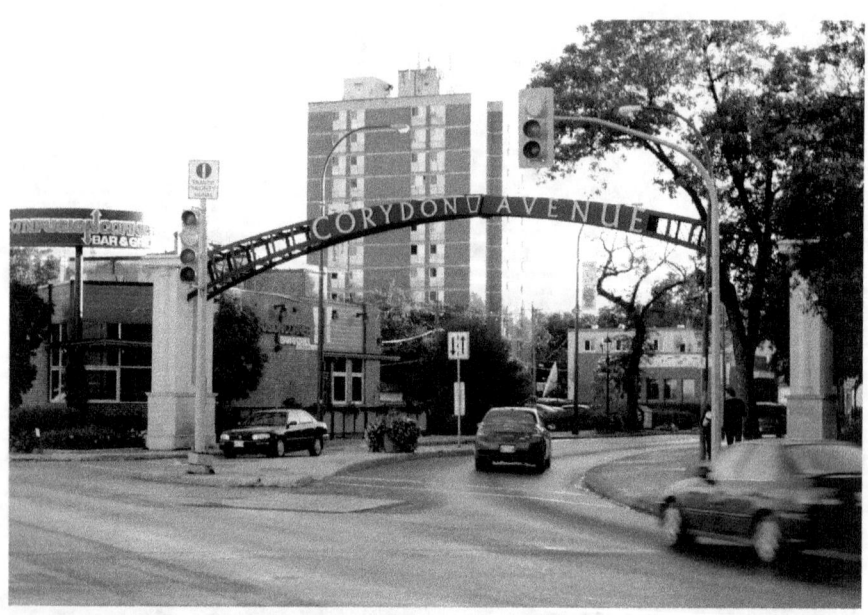

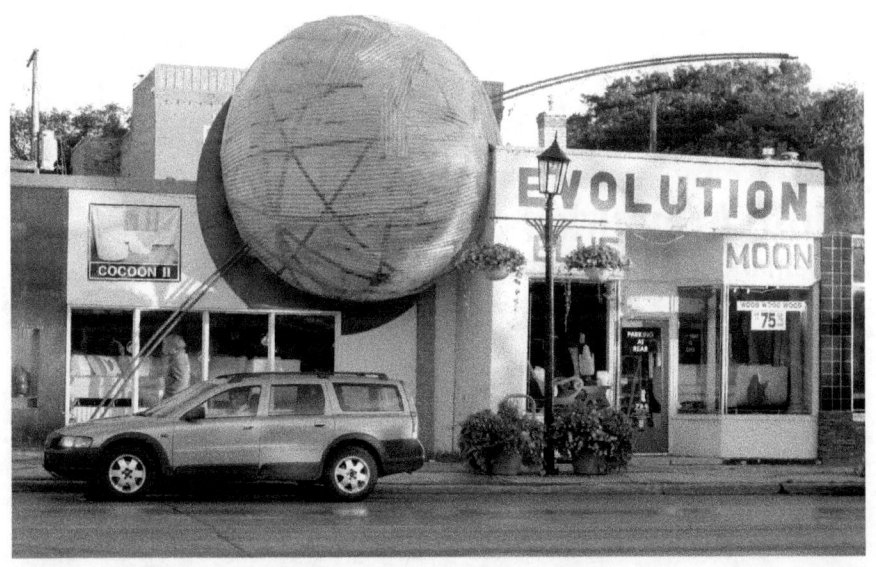

A friend told us a story about a late night Corydon adventure that springs up in our minds often when thinking of this site. He said that one late summer night after drinking a group of friends decided to walk along the rooftops of Corydon. Eventually, they made it to the roof top of the Evolution Moon storefront, and found that in behind the makeshift 3D moon there was an opening big enough to squeeze through. The opening is hidden from the street level, so no one knew they had crawled into the giant sphere. He said that because there was a street light close by that there was a soft glow that let them see the inside where they were sitting and that there was a lot more space in the moon then you would think from just looking up at it on the sidewalk.

Minto Armouries
Placemarker 355: 274 Minto St. and St. Mathews Ave.

The Minto Armoury was a site that stumped us until the public provided us with some insight. The armory had a large area of land in a residential area. The armoury building occupied one site of the street, while a large area was fenced up with tall barbed wire fences. The ground was no longer grass, more just dirty, and was used to store several military vehicles. The fenced area seemed to be an intimidating space, something that might be just as intimidating to the residents of the surrounding houses. We would have pinned this site as disliked. However, it was marked as liked. We tried to find reasons why this would be someone's favorite site in Winnipeg. An insightful answer came to us at the Tallest poppy. What seemed to be positive about this site was the armoury's architecture.

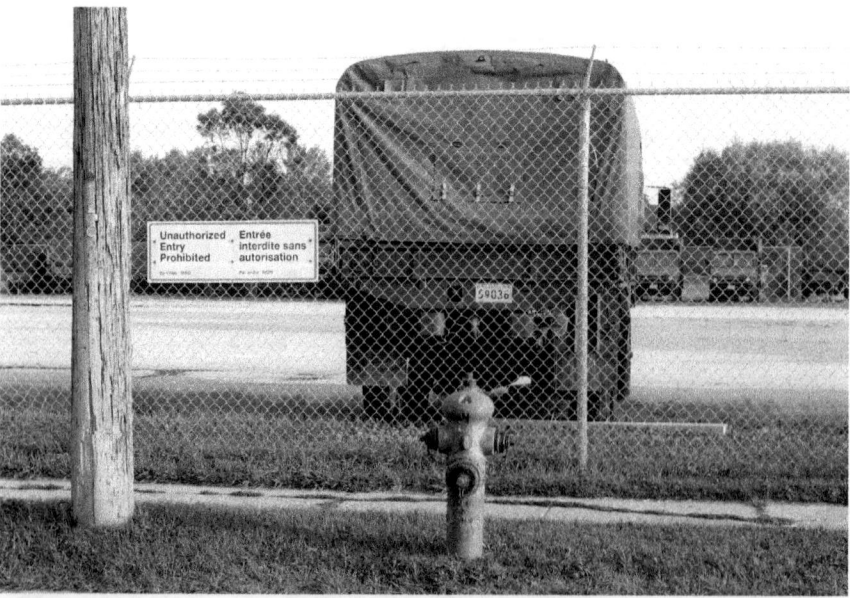

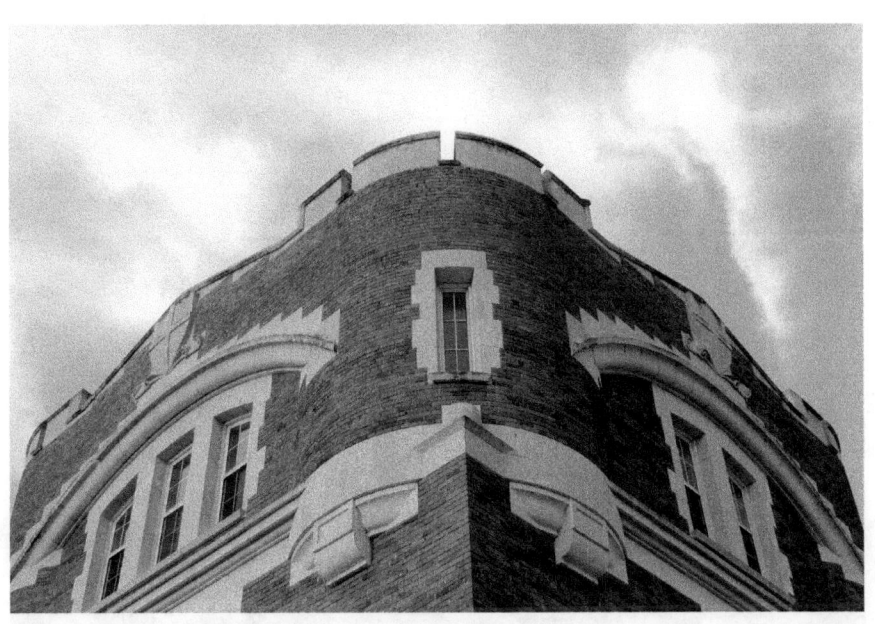

Please choose a dot on the map or a photo on the wall and tell us what you think of it.

Location: Minto Armory

Liked/Disliked:

Why: Looks like a castle in the heart of the West End. ~~They~~ ~~would~~ I'd love to build a moat of landscaping (Piet Douf style prairie garden) fit for a knight & a maiden.

University of Manitoba

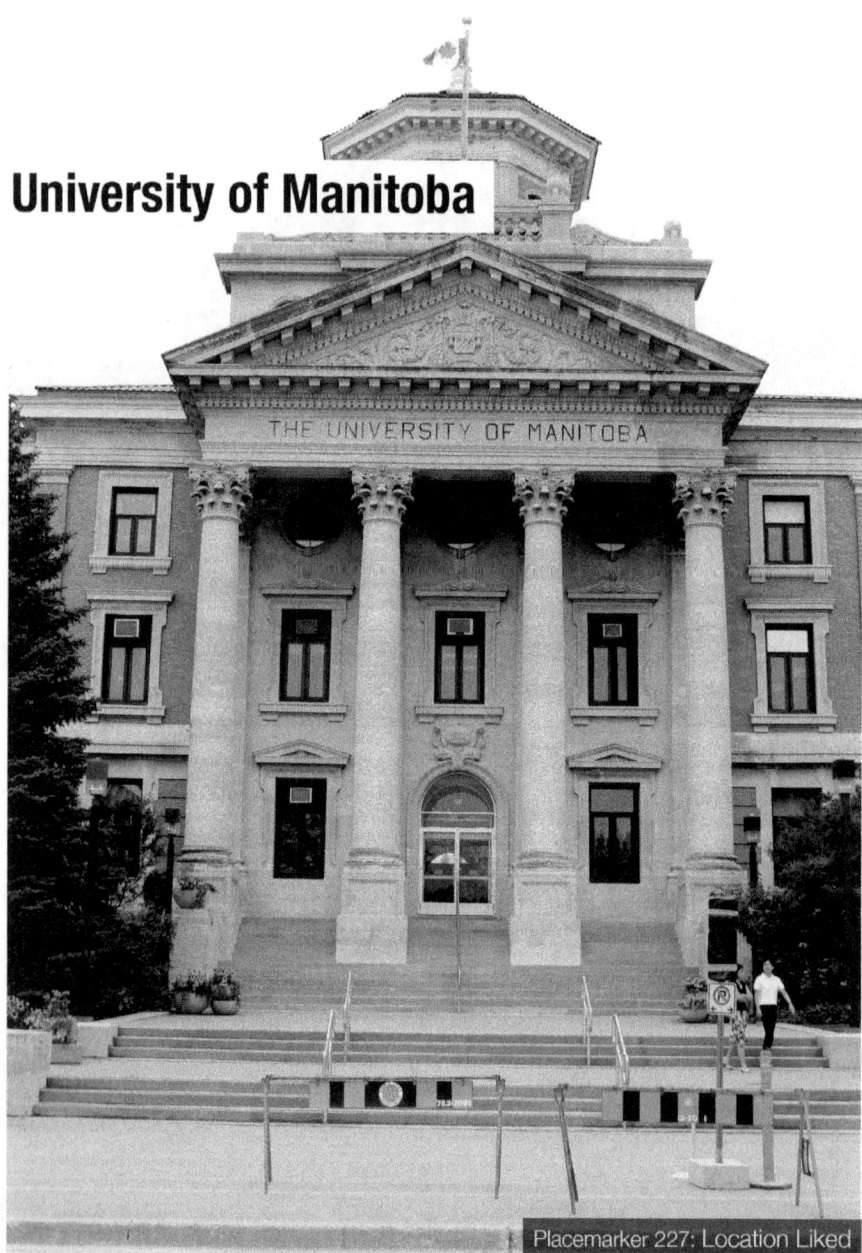

Placemarker 227: Location Liked

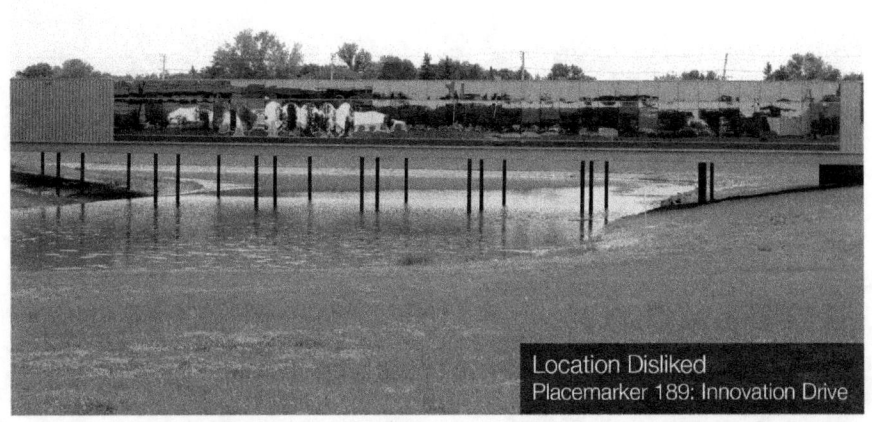

Location Disliked
Placemarker 189: Innovation Drive

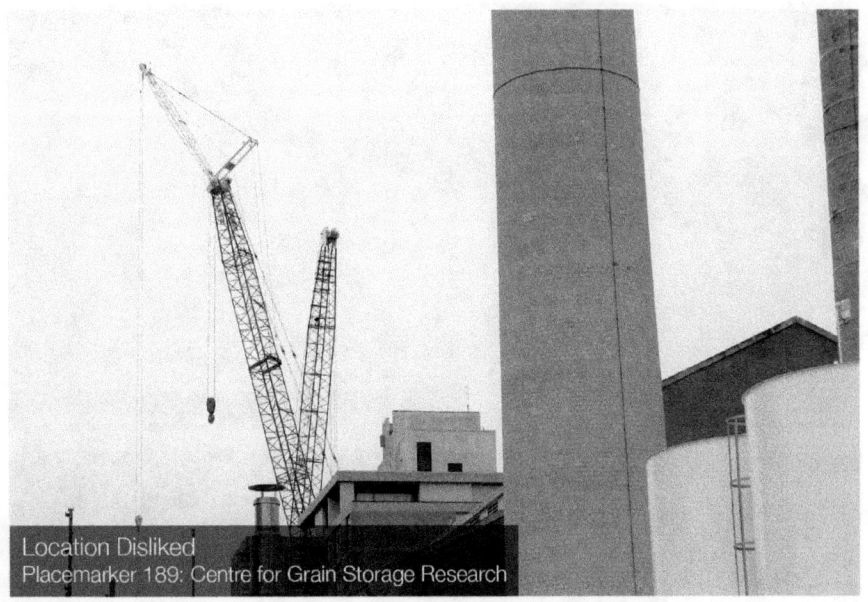

Location Disliked
Placemarker 189: Centre for Grain Storage Research

42

Winnipeg Airport
Placemarker 74/75/105/253/261/313/382/383/384/385/422

Located at the far east side of town is this generally favoured site where business and travel trips are put into motion. Large tourist advertisments greet new arrivals with images of open-eyed gambler gazing at brightly lit dices and slot machine. The James Armstrong International airport is currently in a transitional phase, a new terminal is being built northeast from the present location. The goal to the expansion is to attract wider-bodied aircrafts, and add new routes to Europe to their itinerary. According to CTV's Jeremy Hunka the first stage of the expansion will not be completed until 2011 due to some unexpected complications.

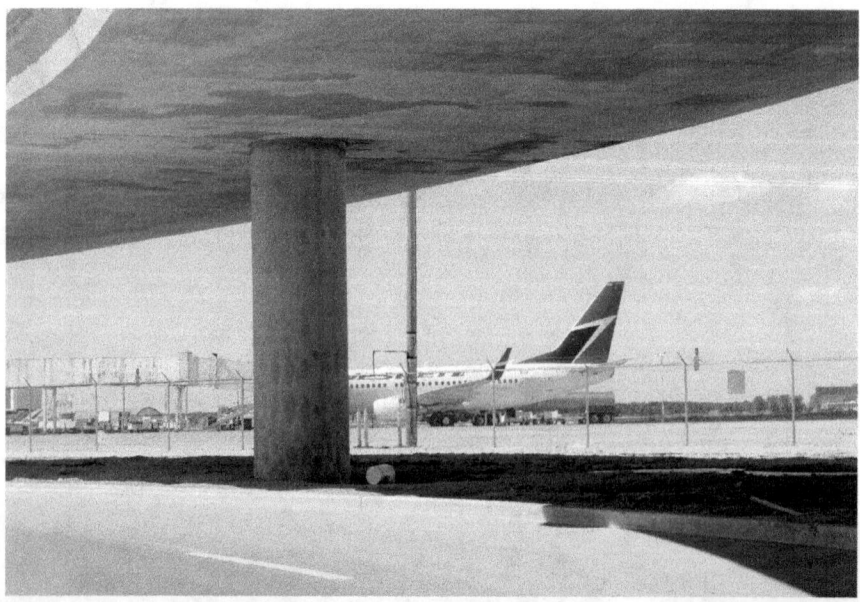

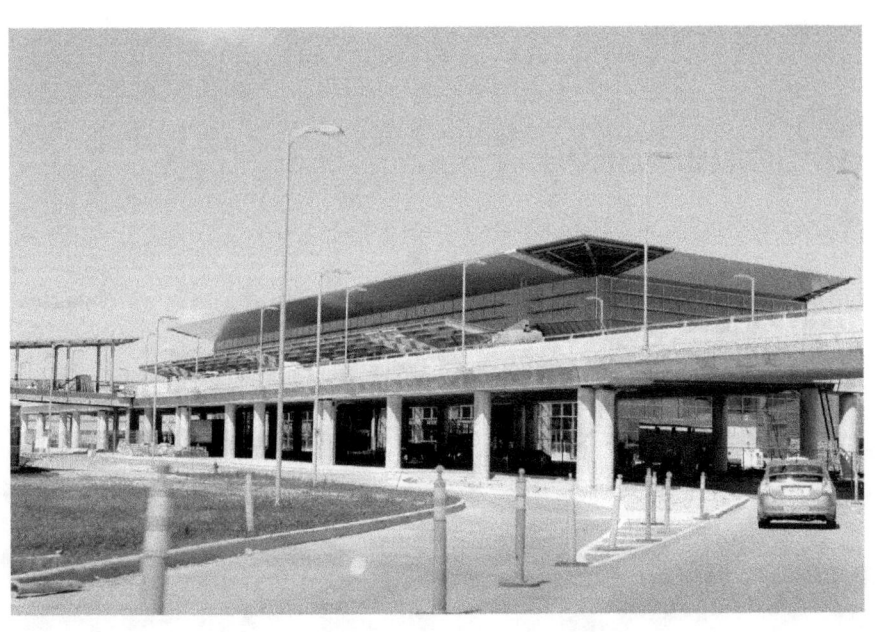

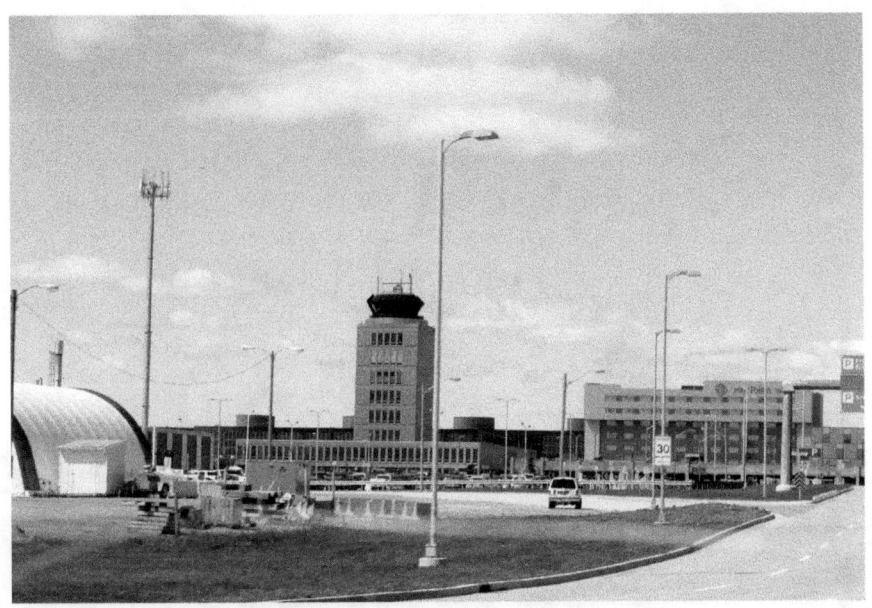

44

Chapter Two
Relocated Sites

A couple of sites are vacant storefronts and buildings due to franchise re-locations and re-development choices. What is remains are empty structures with skeletal signs and dismantled insides.

The Safeway at Ellice Ave. and Wall St. has been closed for two years now due to the franchise's decision to invest in a "Super-Safeway" by highway 90, located in a former Hooter's establishment. Due to the lack of interest in renovating the site, it's original structure that was designed in the 60s remains intact. Instilling a sense of nostalgia of an aesthetic from a past generation.

Similar to this empty grocery store the location of the former Manitoba Public Insurance Company remains inactive with several signs marking it's re-location. The design of the buildings was made specifically for automotive inspections.

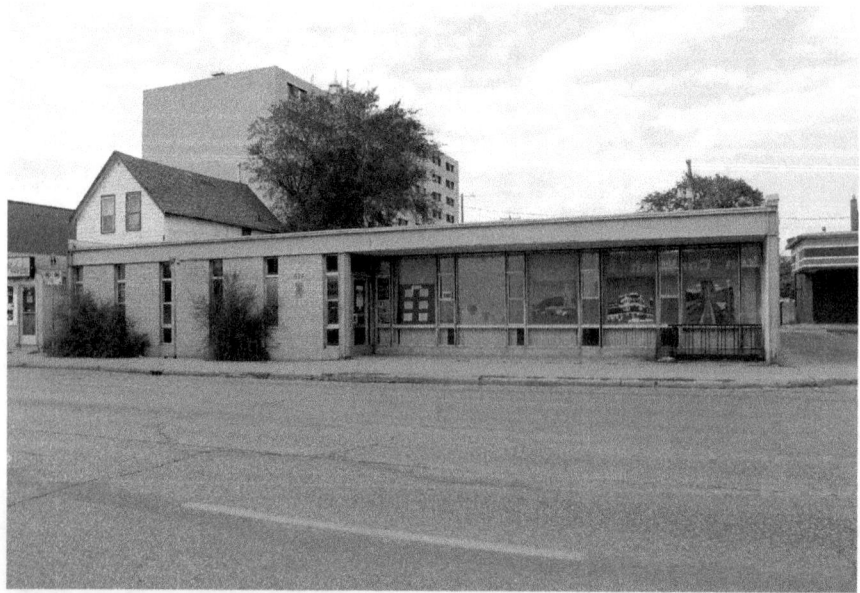

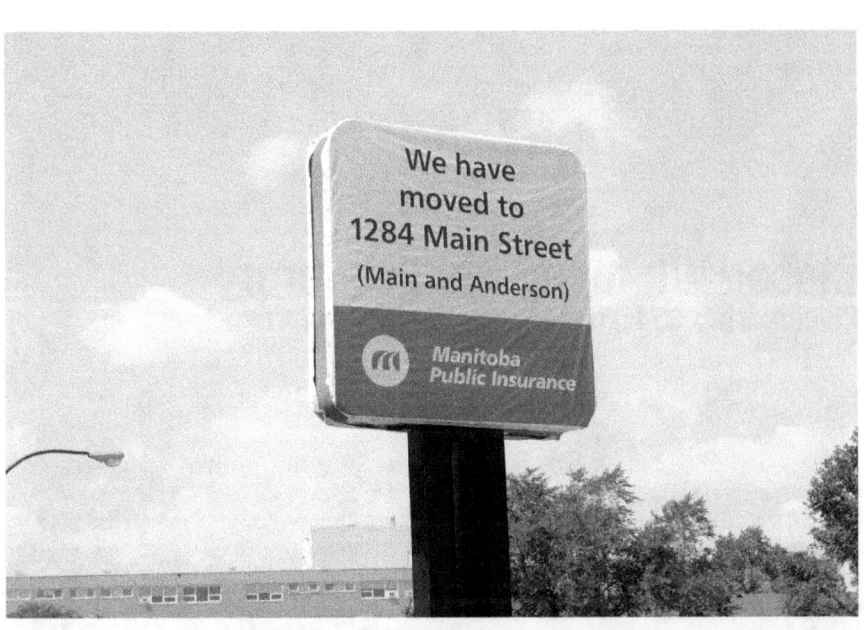

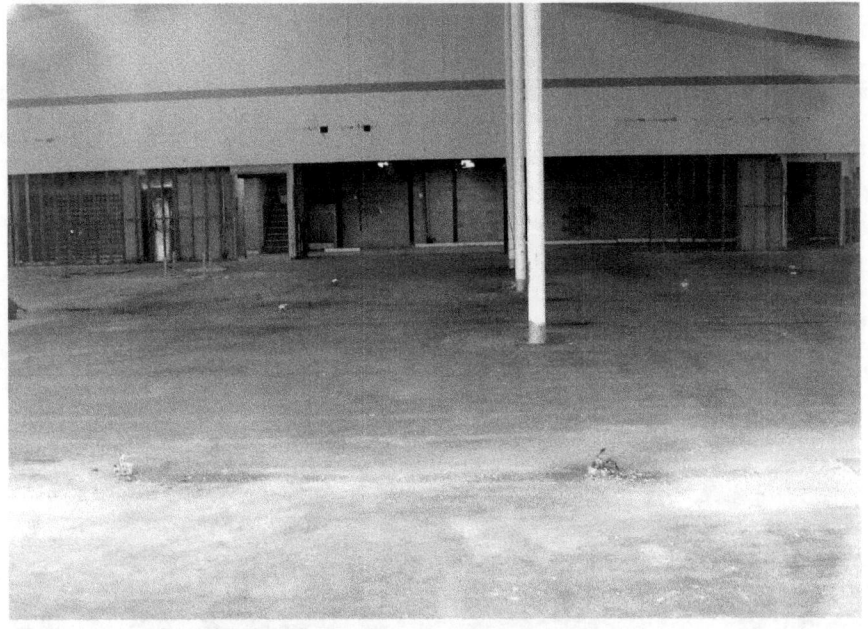

Closed Winnipeg Public Library
Placemarker 354: Ellice Ave. and Arlington St.

The old West End Public Library is located on Ellice and Arlington, right beside a seven-eleven convenience store. The building is completely bare, the shelves filled with collected books and the literary source have been removed. The sign has been stripped and all that is left is an imprint on the metal beam spelling out "Winnipeg Public Library." The large glass windows are dirty, unwashed and beyond the glass are the dusty empty floors of the vacant building. Looking passed the closed/moved signs, there is a tiny sticker marking Winnipeg's Centennial from 1874-1974. The remnants of an establishment's past structure leaves us questioning it's future role or identity, what will this building become?

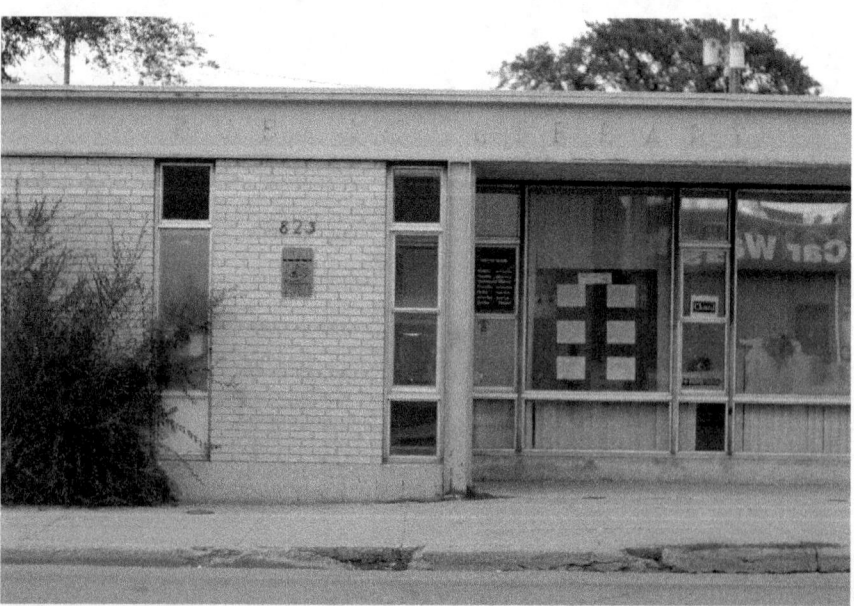

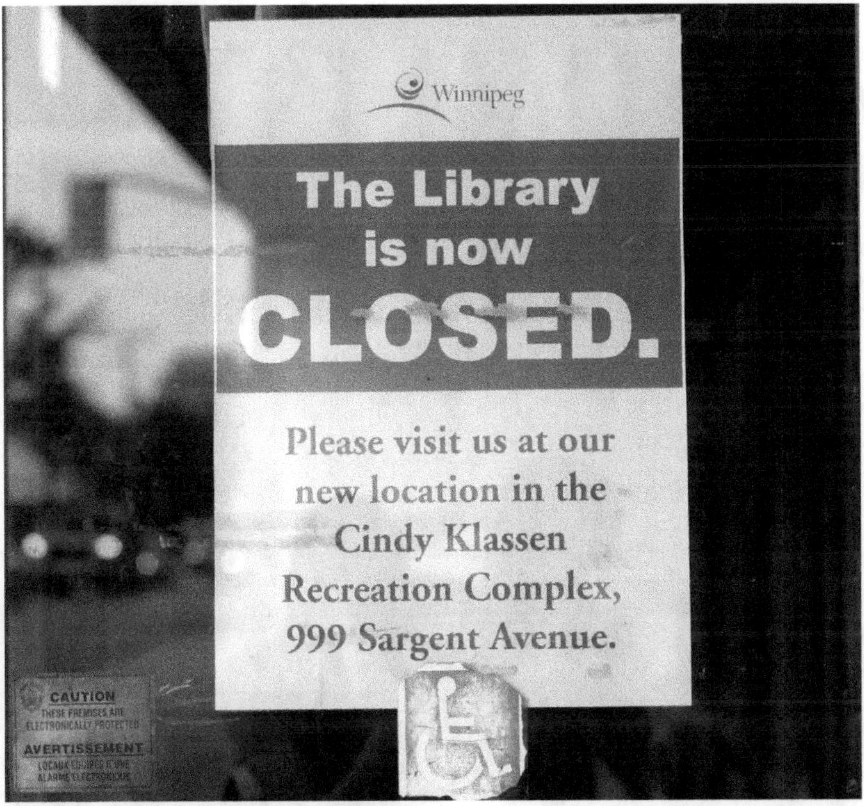

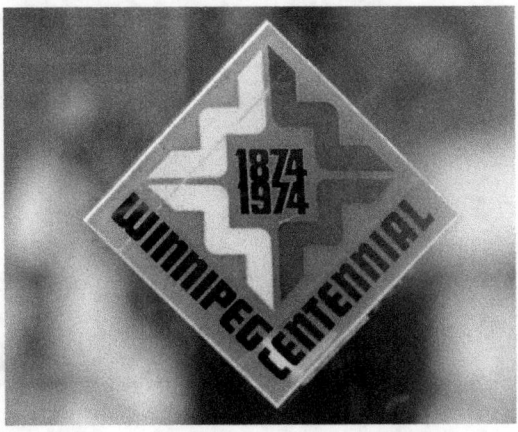

The library has re-located to the Cindy Klassen Recreation Centre, where they are in a larger and newly developed facility. With the move they have also increased their working hours due to the expansion of the establishment.

Closed Safeway in the West End
Placemarker 193: Ellice Ave. and Wall St.

On December 10th, 2008 the Safeway at Ellice and Wall St. closed it's doors for good. What remains is this empty lot, an abandoned building, and a tall dismantled sign. This large parking lot is covered with tire tread marks directing customers to each exit point. Taking a peak through these large window panes one can see the bare walls and pillars of a once busy grocery store.

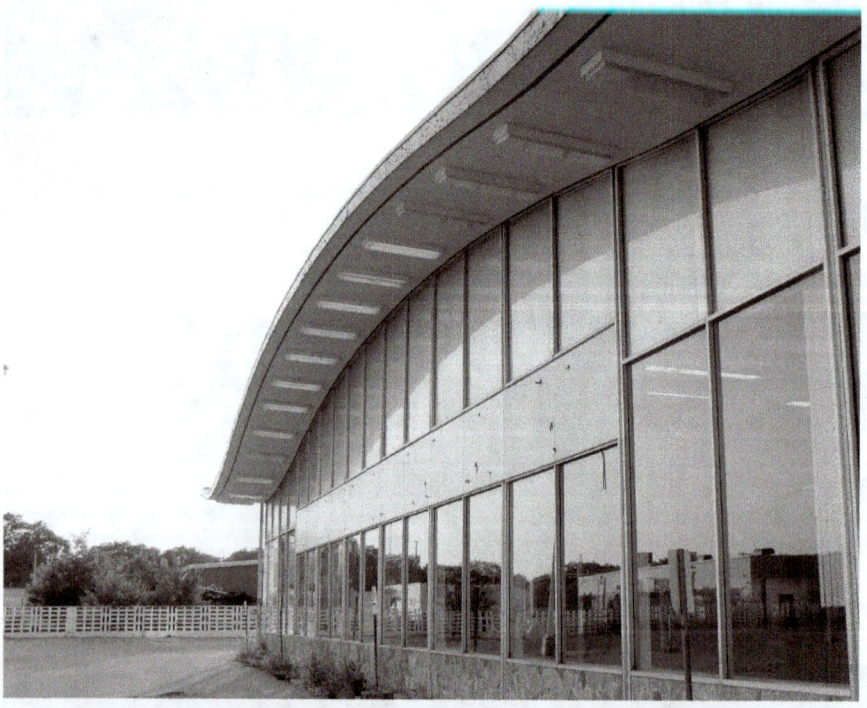

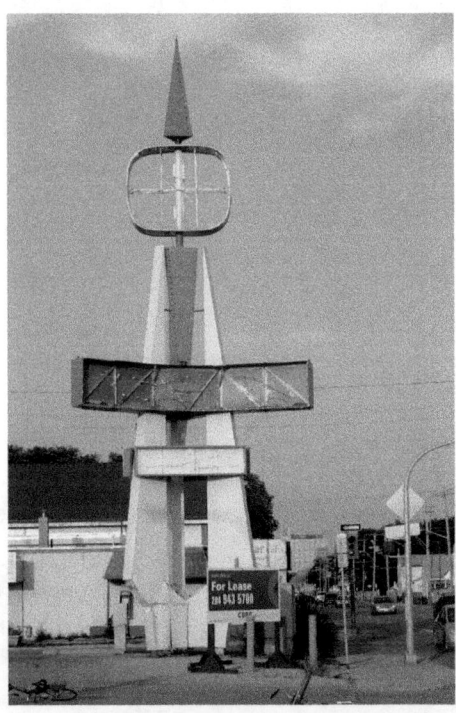

This branch is located within an inner-city community. It is now shutdown due to it's poor performance, and the high costs to give the structure a face-lift. The next location that is the closest to the west end is situated at Polo Park and is now closed as well. The company has decided to favour and develop a new 'Super' Safeway at Ness by Route 90 within an old "Hooters location."

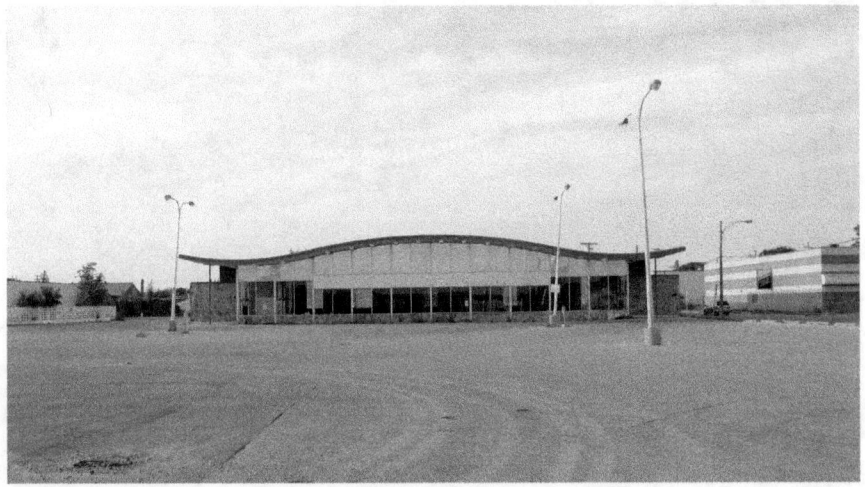

Empty Lot
Placemarker 37: Simcoe St. and Ellice Ave.

On the corner of Ellice and Simcoe, sits this empty lot. There is an eerie silence over the space, which is strange as it borders on Ellice. All that can be heard are the bells of a nearby church, ringing out the chorus of Alleluia. The area is gated and all that remains are disintegrating concrete blocks. A set of deep tire tracks are left in the sandy ground, possibly from before the fence was put up. The skeleton of a real estate sign is toppled over and it now faces the ground. It's as though there is no hope left for this site, left to be taken over by brush and gated from pedestrians.

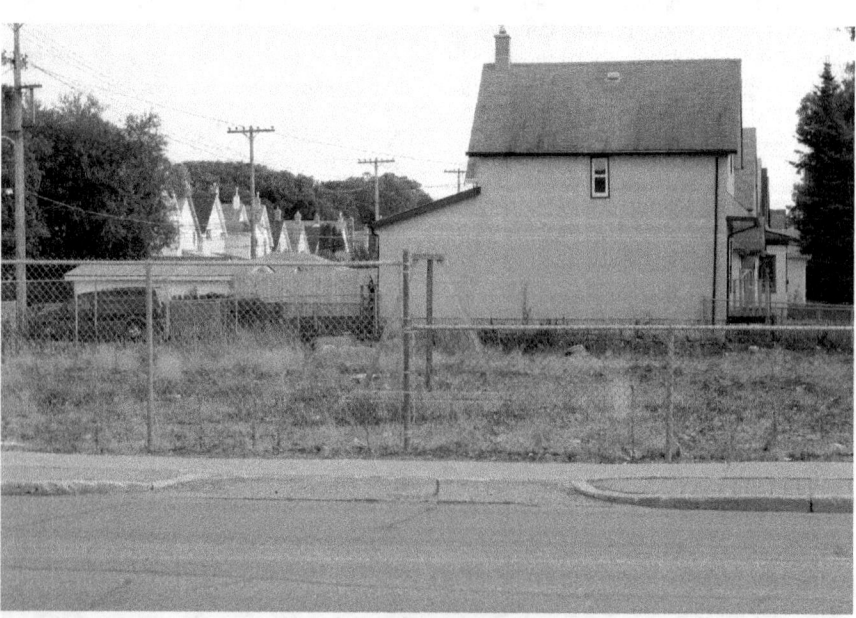

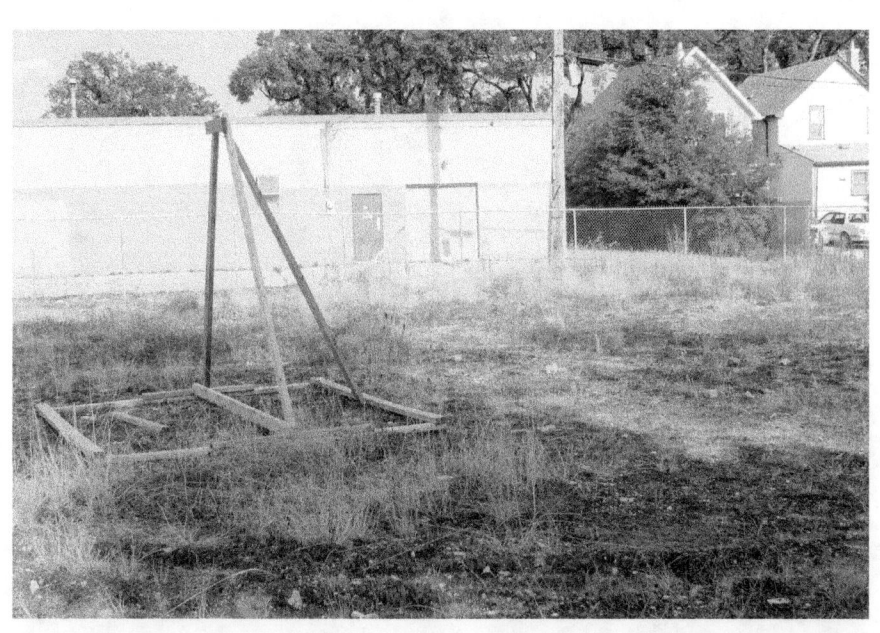

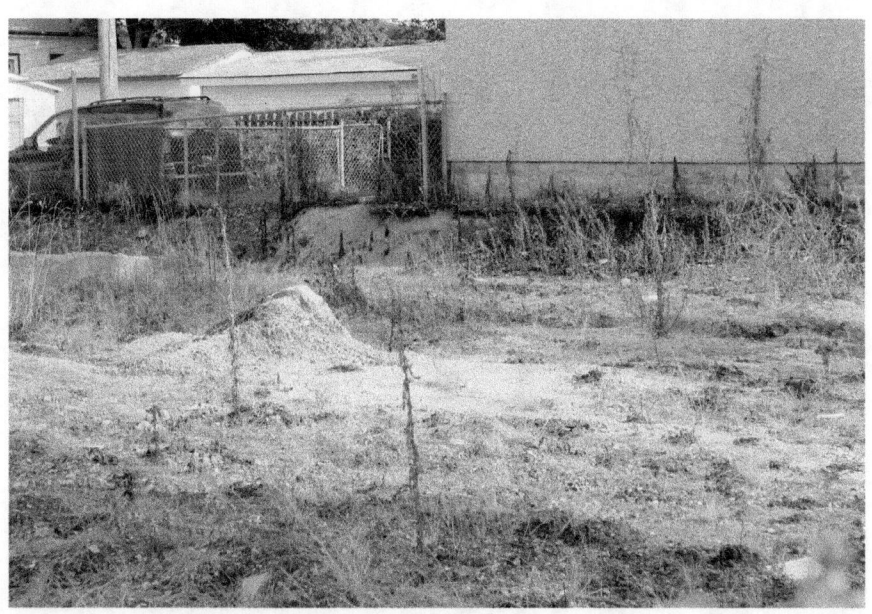

Speedy Auto Garage
Placemarker 344: Sherbrook St. and Portage Ave.

The Speedy Auto garage was one of the many unique sites we have visited. Once a church or perhaps an old fire station, it was converted into an auto garage and is now boarded up and abandoned. It was a strange sight, seeing a large Speedy sign tacked onto the side of the tower of this building. The sign now draws the viewer's eye directly to it, rather than the beautiful detailed architecture that makes up the tower.

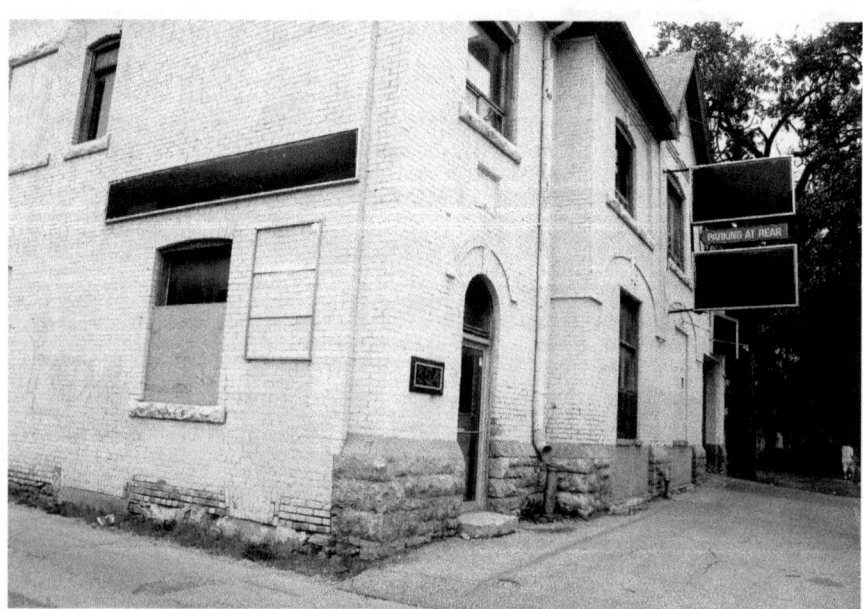

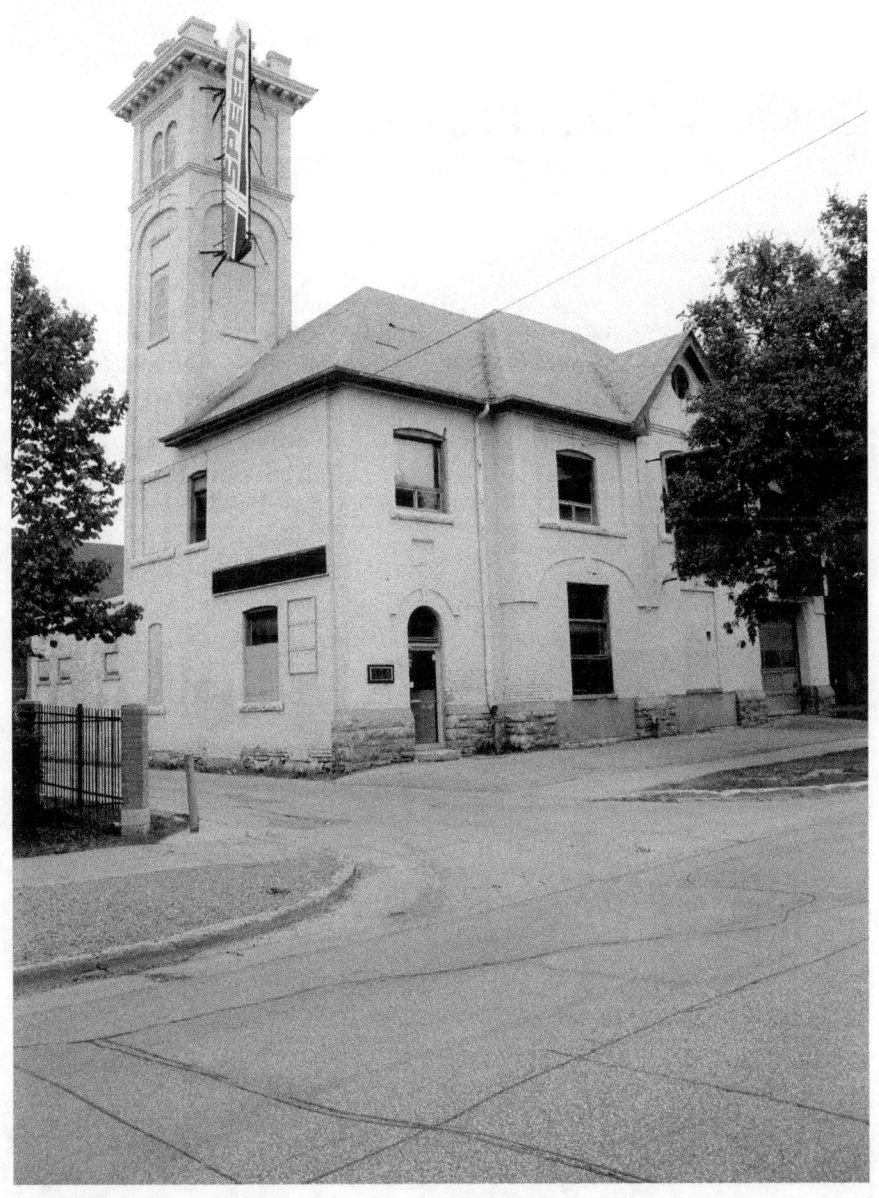

Closed Gateway Packers
Placemarker 358: Sutherland Ave. and Maple St.

Nestled beside the tracks, the closed Gateway Packers waits for it's next company to inhabit the building. The structure has been passed down a long line of industrial businesses. Built in 1874, the building was first known as Vulcan Iron Works and "begun as a two man operation with John Mckechnie and W.W. McMilan...The plant in the years since then has produced all sorts of steel products much of it for CPR's Weston shops."(Thompson p.21) The indestructible nature of this structure is apparent, seeing as it's damage is only on the surface. However, for now it sits, bare brick spotting through a thin coat of white paint, collecting graffiti tags.

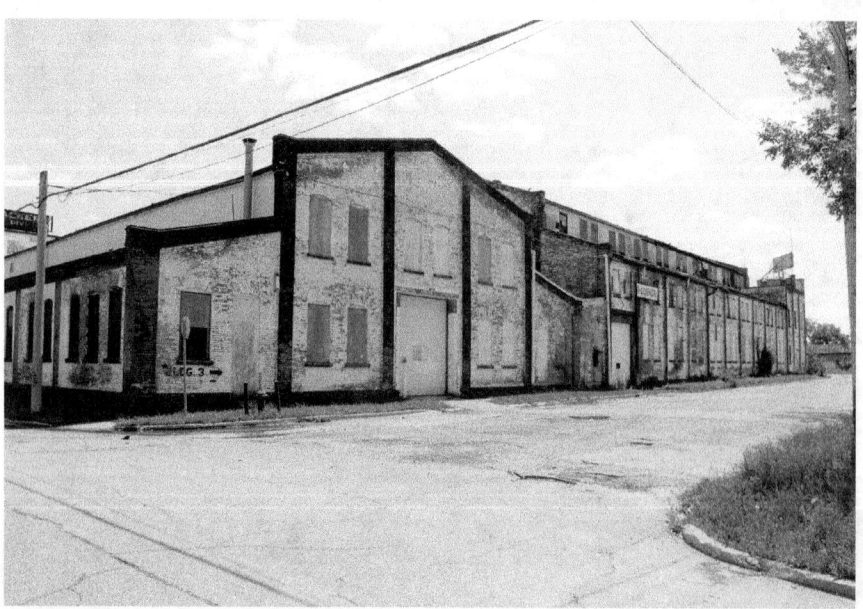

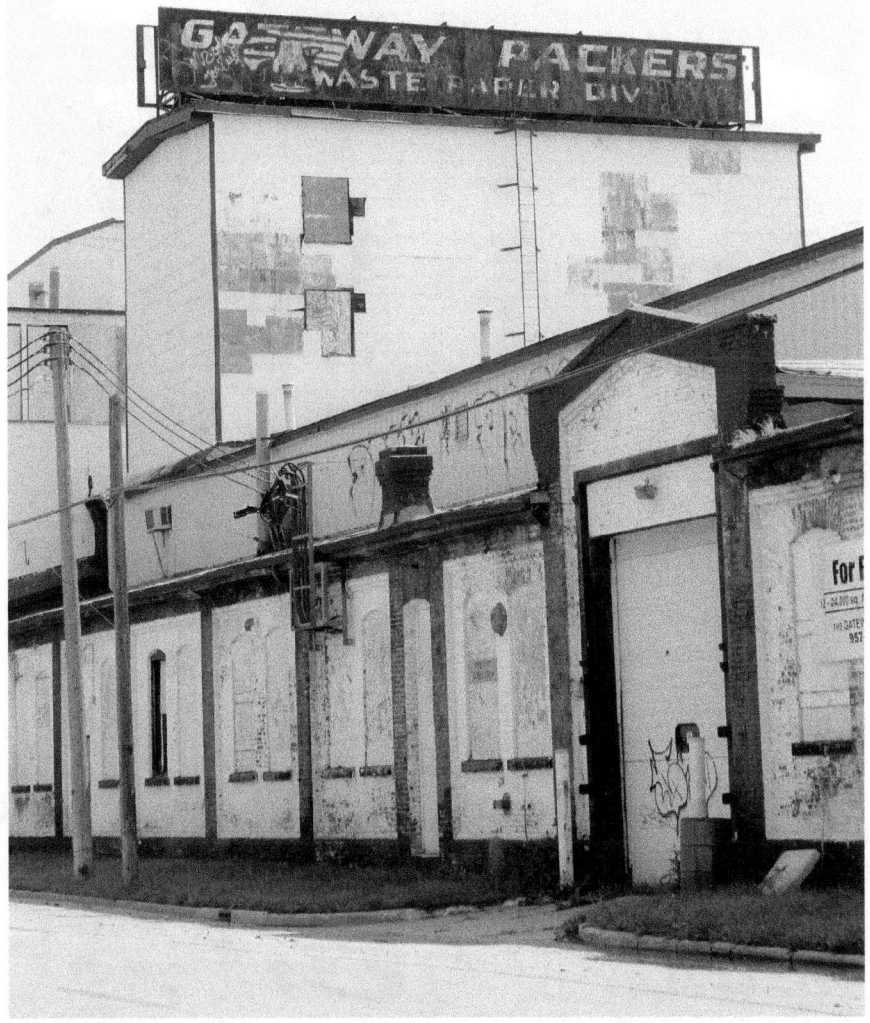

Chapter Three

Pedestrian Feedback

Some sites were directly linked to issues of mobility to the pedestrian. This was not a surprise since we strategically placed our flyers in areas of heavy foot traffic. Kenaston Boulevard seemed to completely disregard pedestrians and prioritize vehicles. This intersection also creates a belittling effect on a pedestrian, surrounded by the "dysfunction of strip-malls" a local writes, a site enveloped by the consumption of franchise rather than community.

The pedestrian walkway at Portage and Main St. was closed since 1976, due to an agreement between the city and private developers. It did open an underground pathway linking the existing shopping malls at each four corners and allowing foot traffic beneath the busy streets. These tunnels are also linked up with the sky-walk within the downtown core. Even though the agreement spawn through commercial incentives, it does provide a comfortable alternative during the winter season. However, if a pedestrian's intention is simply to cross the street, the detour may prove to be an inconvenience.

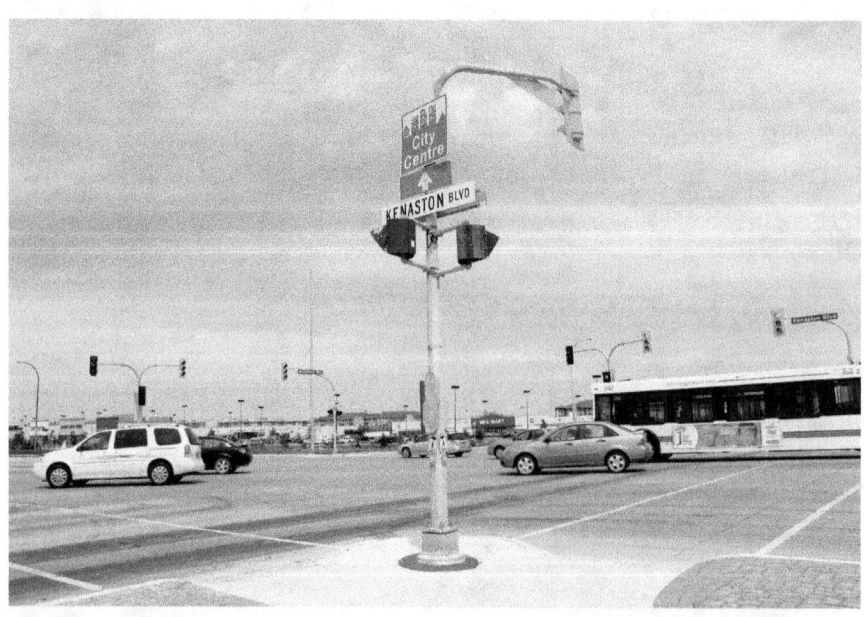

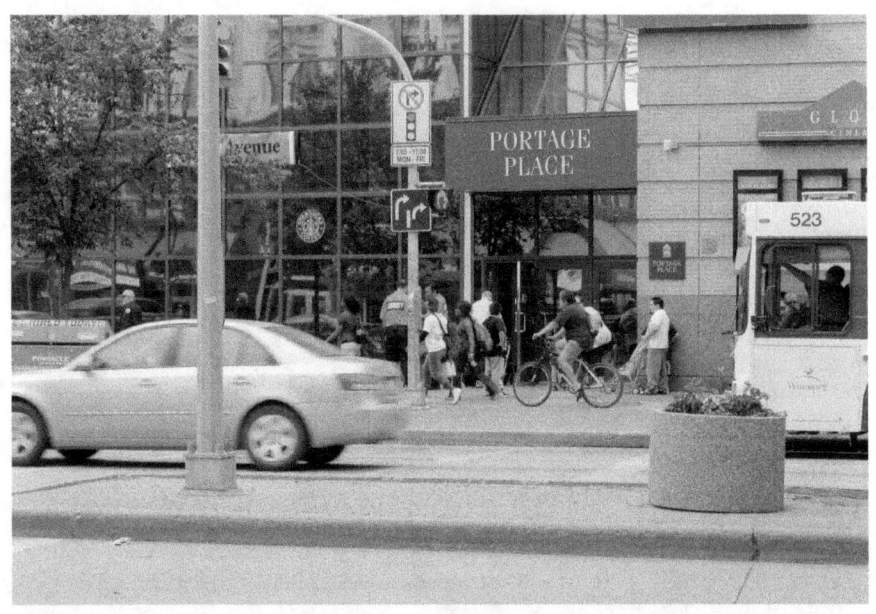

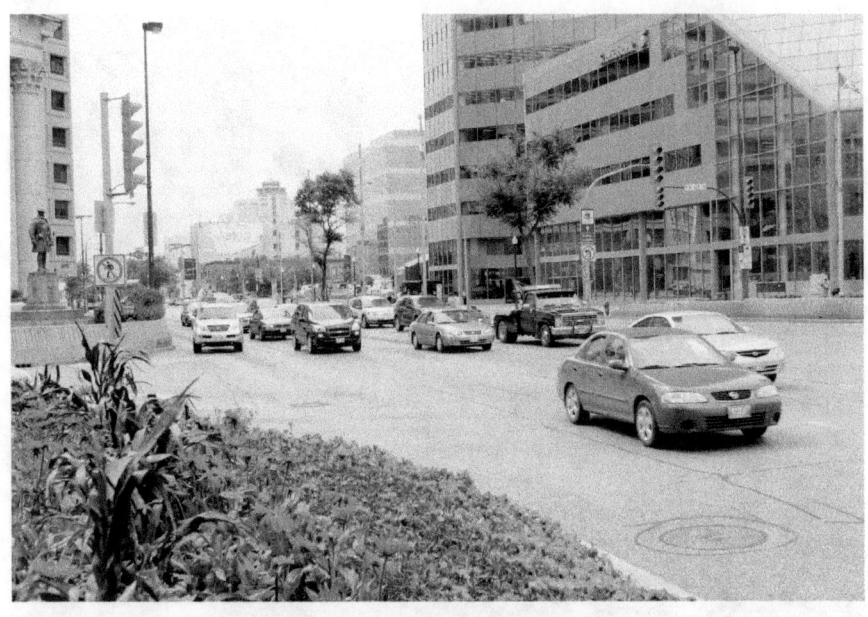

"Tree Children" Sulpture by Leo Mol
Placemarker 3 and 311: Main St. and Portage Ave.

Portage and Main St., is an infamous Winnipeg street corner in Canada. Country singers such as Neil Young and Stomping Tom Corners, have written song about it's social and economic prosperity, also mentioning it's below 40 degree Celsius winters. The intersection acted as a hub for the city's main transportation routes and was once the centre for the banking industry in Western Canada. Numerous festivals & parades have occurred at this location, as well as the Winnipeg General Strike of 1919.

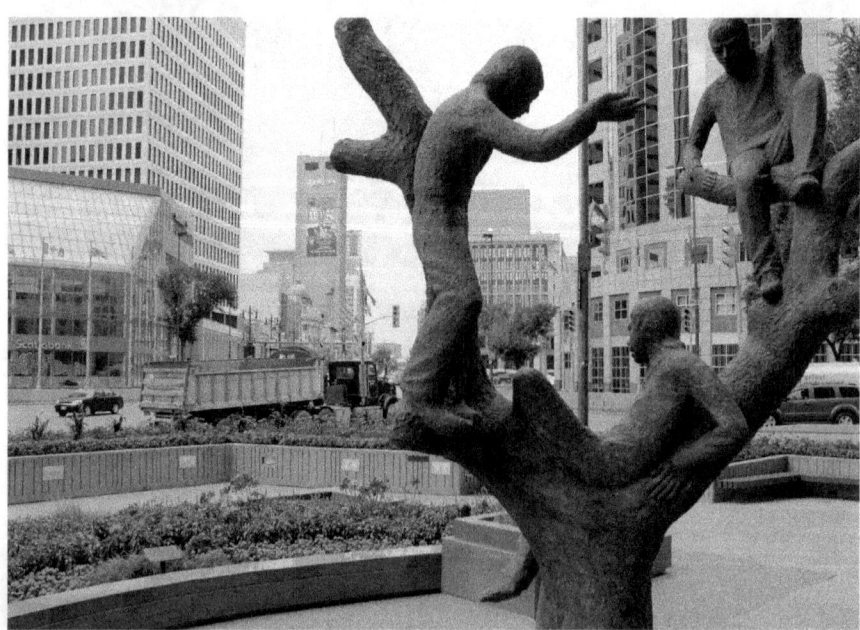

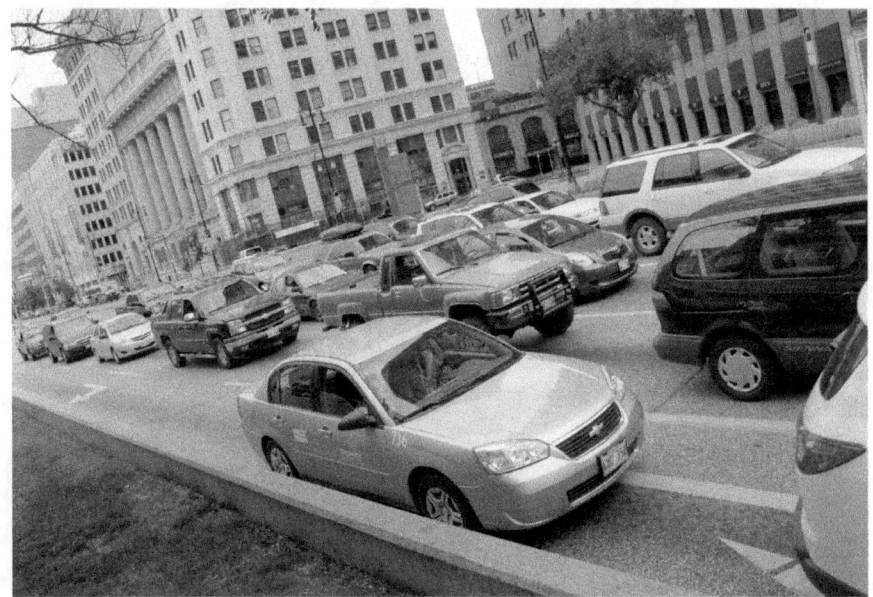

In 1976, the city of Winnipeg signed an agreement with private developers to close the pedestrian pathway, and open an underground pathway to link up shopping mall at each corner. You can access the sky-walk from these tunnel and walk across a good portion of the downtown area.

Looking at it today one can be overwhelmed with the rapid car flow at the intersection. Very few locals can remember crossing this intersection during the day, or have had a chance. A sculpture made by Leo Mol of Children in a treetop, it overlooks this street corner reminding us of those playful days and celebrating this once approachable area.

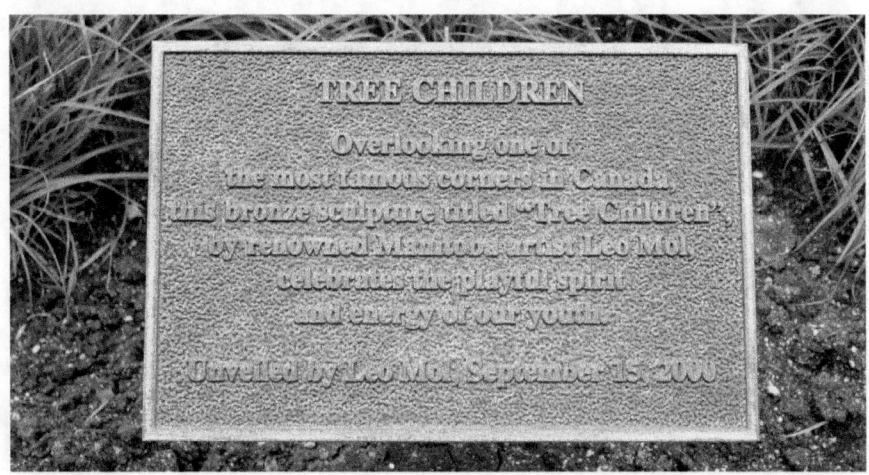

Kenaston Boulevard
Placemarker 347: Kenaston Blvd. and McGillivray Blvd.

This site is the intersection of two busy boulevards that are surrounded by strip-malls and outlet stores. This area of consumption, is used by the surrounding sub-urbs of Whyte Ridge and Linden Woods. Traffic at the intersection is predominately cars and city buses. There are button-operated crosswalks; however they didn't seem to be functional and it never seems to be safe to cross the four-by-four lane highway.

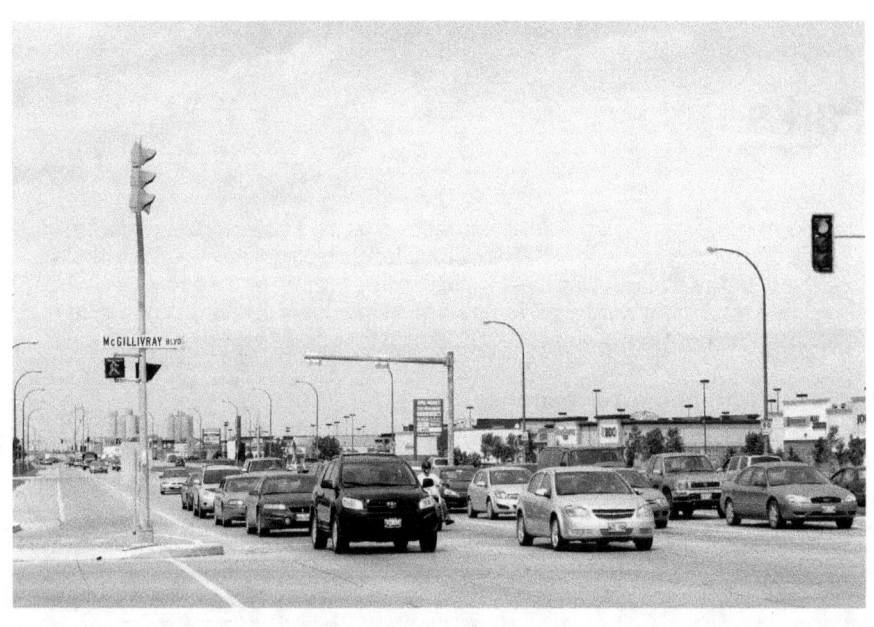

Please choose a dot on the map or a photo on the wall and tell us what you think of it.

Location: KENASTON & McGilvery

Liked/(Disliked):

Why: When I ride by this area I am saddened by the sprawl, the Big Box backyards and dis-function of strip-mall Sub-urbs.

Chapter Four
Parks

Parks also generated a lot of clustering, these sites were also very easy to locate on a map and during field research. The clusters for each park were also clearly liked or disliked. Before documenting these sites, we were puzzled by the strong positive or negative reactions towards certain parks. We assumed a park is a park. However, upon visiting each park it was clear that each once possessed it's own character.

Parks with negative responses
Leon Bell, Muys and Don Smith park had clear negative reactions amongst participants. Visiting these parks, it was clear that the negativity was based off of issues of maintenance and upkeep. Don Smith Park, the play structure was unusable to children in the neighborhood. Plywood boarded up openings where slides once where, any wood was badly weathered and splintering. Both Leon Bell and Muys had self-contained bodies of water. Both parks we littered with trash. Stagnant water collecting trash, and algae emitted a foul smell. Grassy areas were covered with geese feces. Muys park also had an additional problem of graffiti on bridge structures.

Parks with positive responses
On the other hand sites that had positive responses such as Assiniboine, Bourkvale and Bruce park, were prosperous and were quite active. Both parks were well maintained, and safe for children to play in. One difference with these parks was that they were being used. The parks with poor maintenance were empty. These parks were crowded and many activities were available for visitors such as Bike paths, Dog schools, lawn bowling, zoos, memorials, fishing, etc. The parks with positive reactions seemed to be a part of the community and in a constant state of renewal. The parks with a negative response seemed to be decorative and with little social function. They also appear to have remained the same since the parks opening.

Parks in re-development
Central park was a positive site. This park is in transitional renovations. A large attempt to make this park family friendly and a resource for the children living the surrounding high-rises. This park is the community gathering place for the neighborhood it is located in. This is an example of taking a park that was a problem area and redeveloping it to create a positive venue for a lower income area. Living across from the park, let us experience firsthand how pivotal this renovation is to it's residents. The renovations opened the site up to ethnic markets, concerts, church services, soccer tournaments and barbecues. Hopefully, this park is setting a positive change in motion.

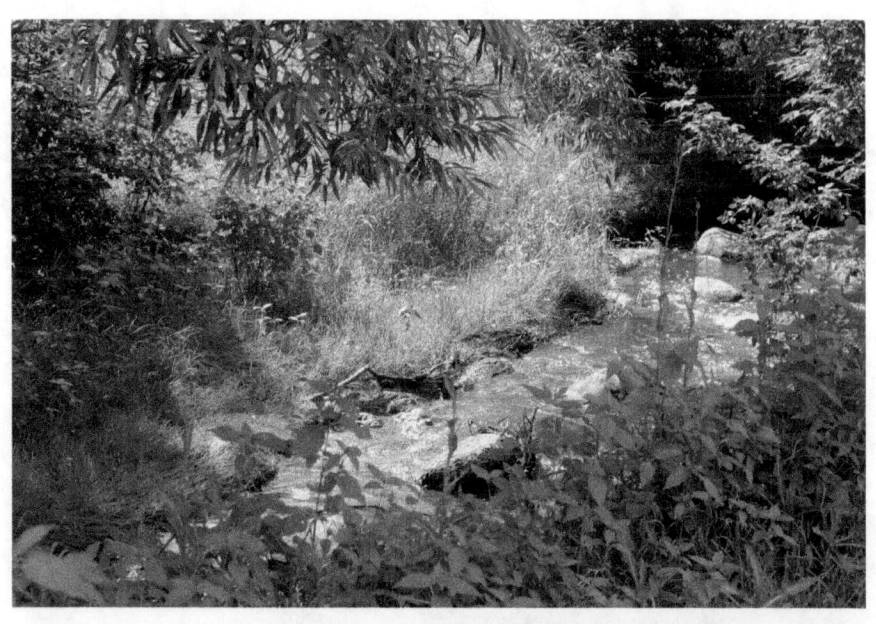

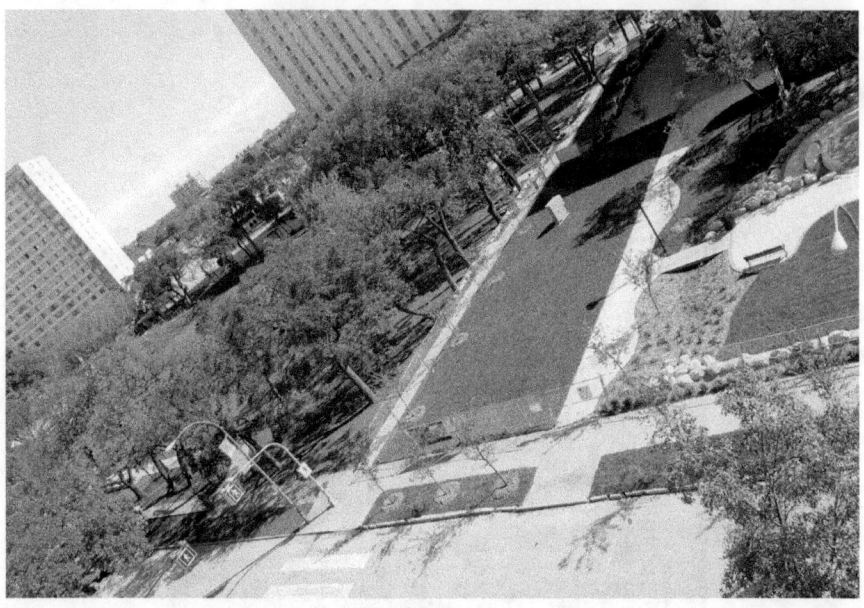

Don Smith Park
Placemarker 161: Scurifield Blvd and Fleetwood Rd

This park has seen better days. The play structure is dated, and does not leave much for the neighbourhood children to play with. Upkeep of the park seems none existent. The spring rockers' wooden seats are weathered and could easily give someone a splinter. The slides are now boarded with plywood.

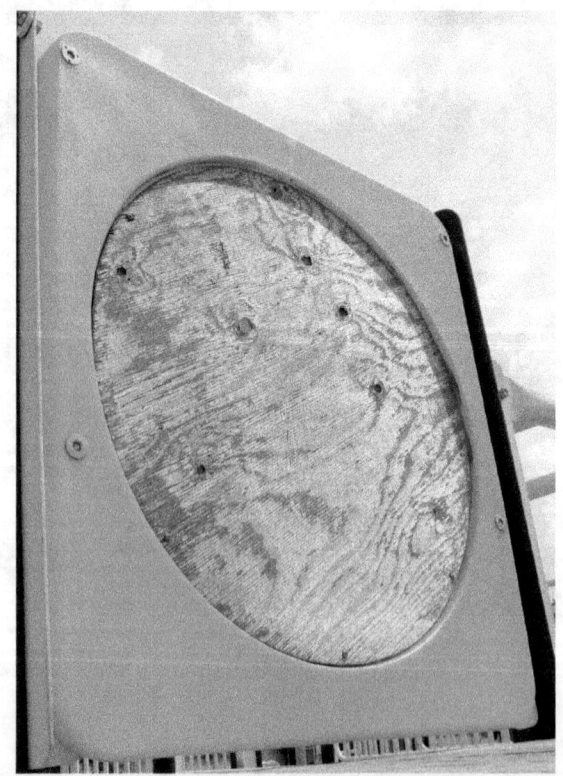

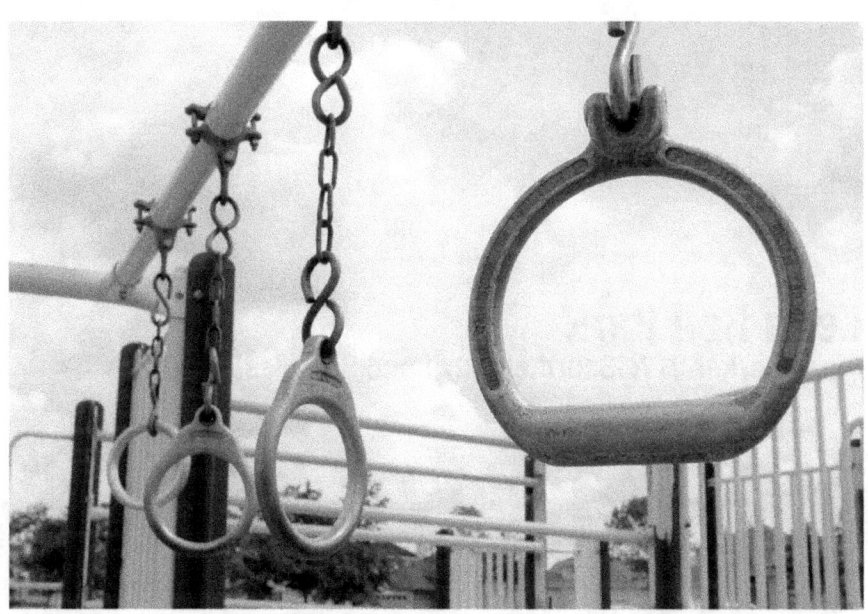

The rings are mismatched and are put together haphazardly. At the edge of the park, planks are missing from the fence, which leads you to a collection of boxcars. The park seems to still be used by the teens and tweens, who once played on the structure in its heyday, as messages of teen love remains in the sand.

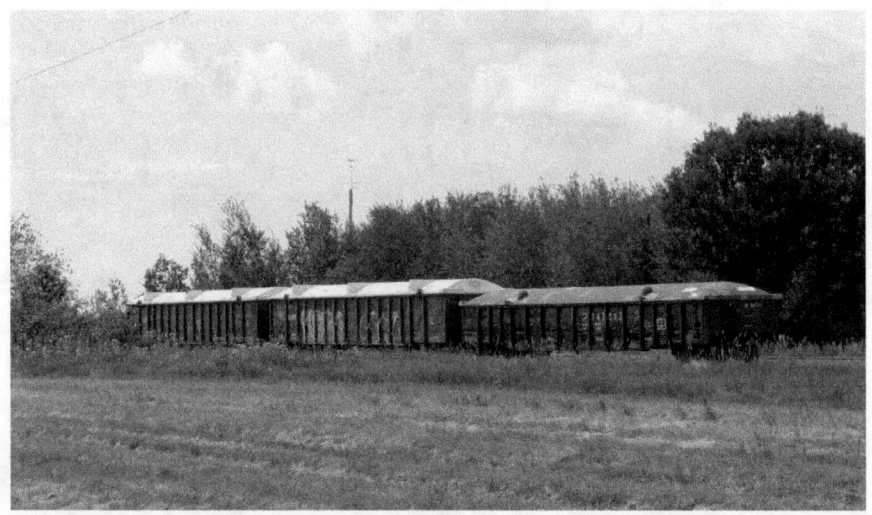

Leon Bell Park
Placemarker 217: Scurifield Blvd and Spindlestone Gate

On the south side of the city this park is located in the richer suburb of Whyte Ridge. Mansions surround the park, their backyards sitting on the edge of the man made pond. A fountain in the centre, and a large pack of geese wander through the yards after their afternoon swim.

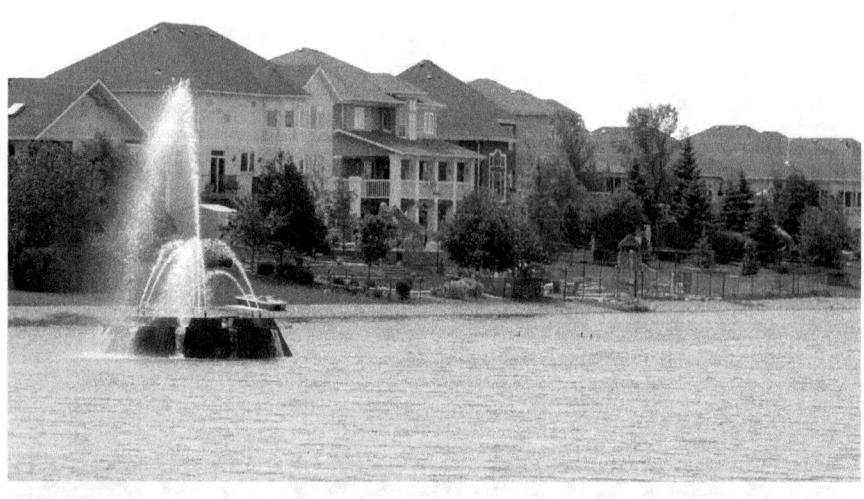

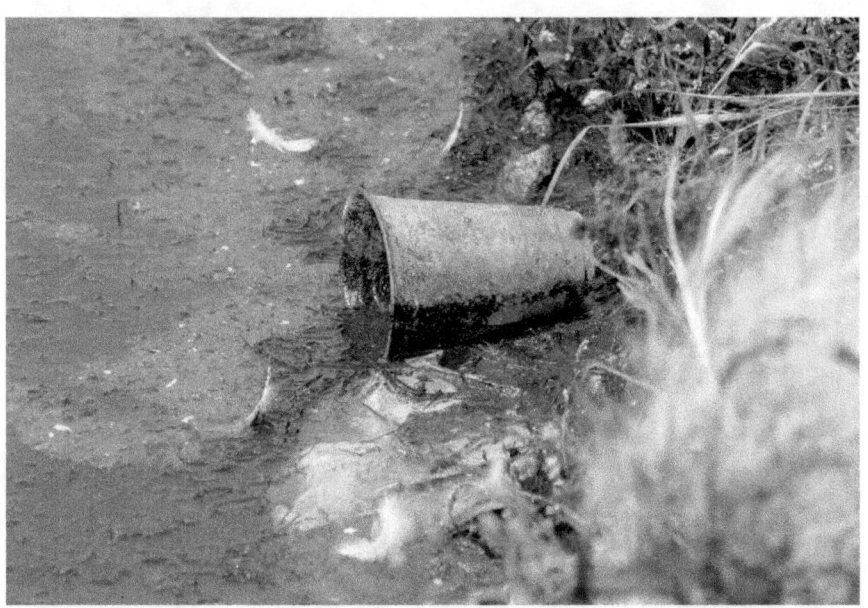

The wind gives the pond a strong current, pushing all the debris and rubble to the edge of the park entrance. The water is stagnant there, with a thick green skin floating on the surface. A strong unpleasant aroma wafts up from the beached trash. At a quick glance this park seems to be a constructed treat, but with a closer look leaves more to be desired.

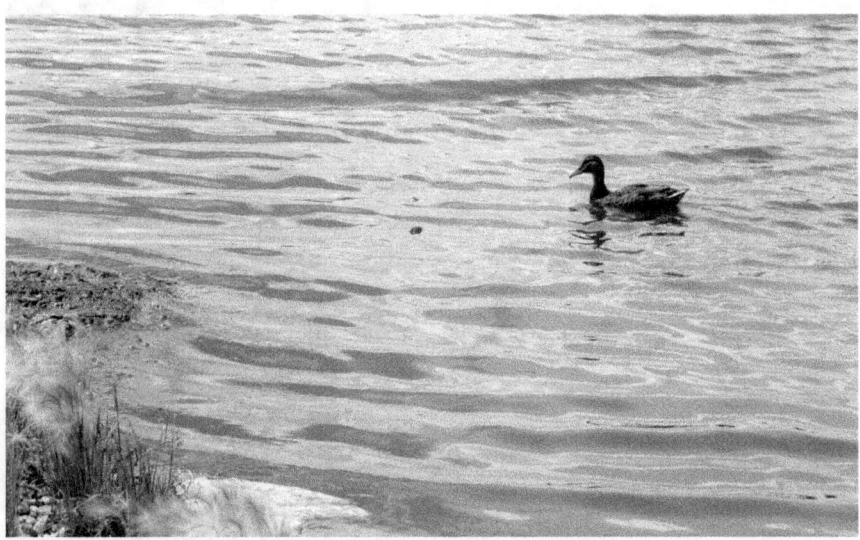

Bourkevale Park
Placemarker 337: Assiniboine Ave. and Ferry Rd.

This park had a positive response towards it. Families filled the park all spending time, training their dog, lawn bowling, or fishing along the edge of the river. The park is well maintained, and the facilities provide many activities that attract the neighbourhood families. A bike path runs through the park that provides joggers and bikers with a trail connecting to Assiniboine and Bruce park.

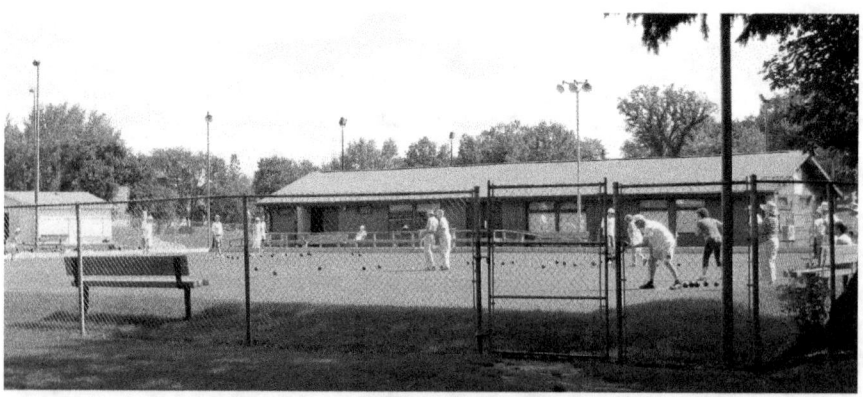

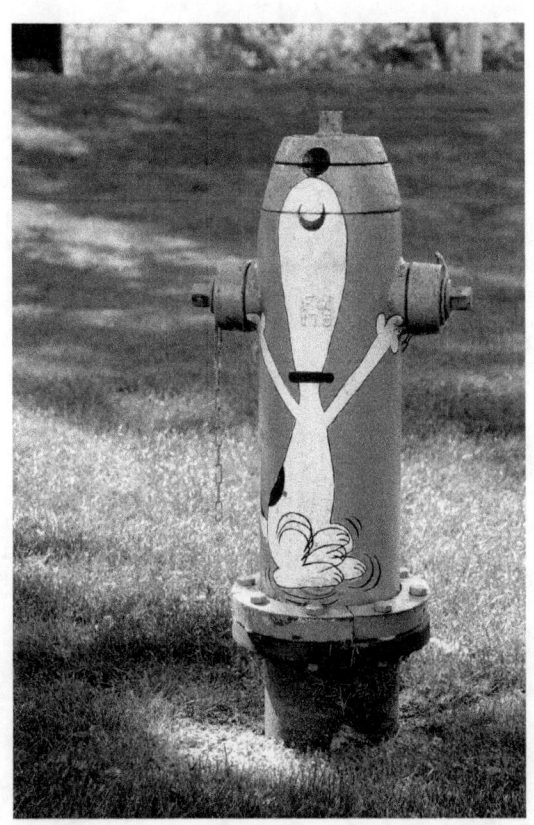

Please choose a dot on the map or a photo on the wall and tell us what you think of it.

Location: Bourkevale Park

Liked/Disliked: Liked

Why: I like when a dull permant object is painted in a cheerful way.

Bruce Park
Placemarker 337: Portage Ave. and Albany St.

Bruce Park has a historic value and was once owned by the Bruce Family. It is south of Portage by Douglas Park Rd. The entrance of the park is surrounded with flowers, and not far from it is a large rock with a plaque telling a little about the site's past. "Peter Bruce once lived on the land and had donated it to the St. James municipality under the conditions it remains green for the locals to enjoy. This promise was discovered by a nine-year old Bailey Herron, while conducting research on his family heritage."

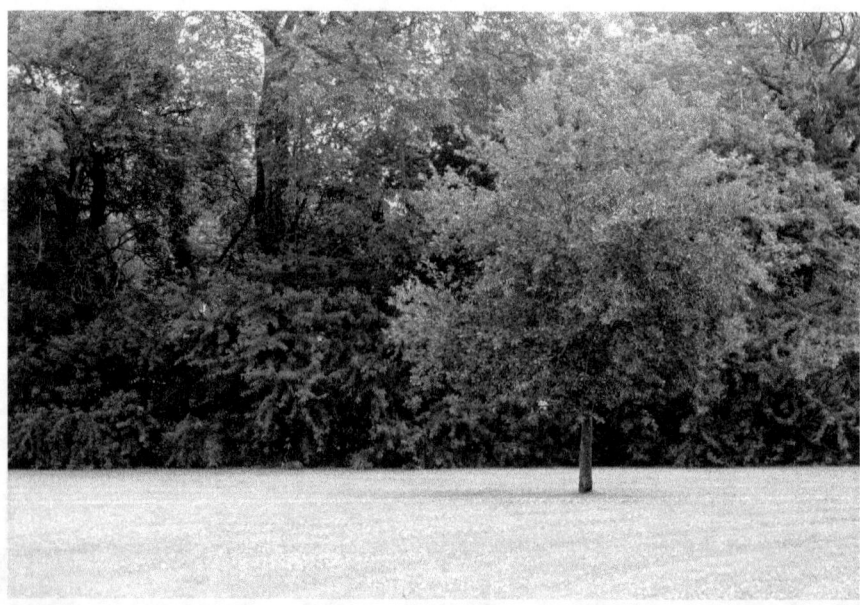

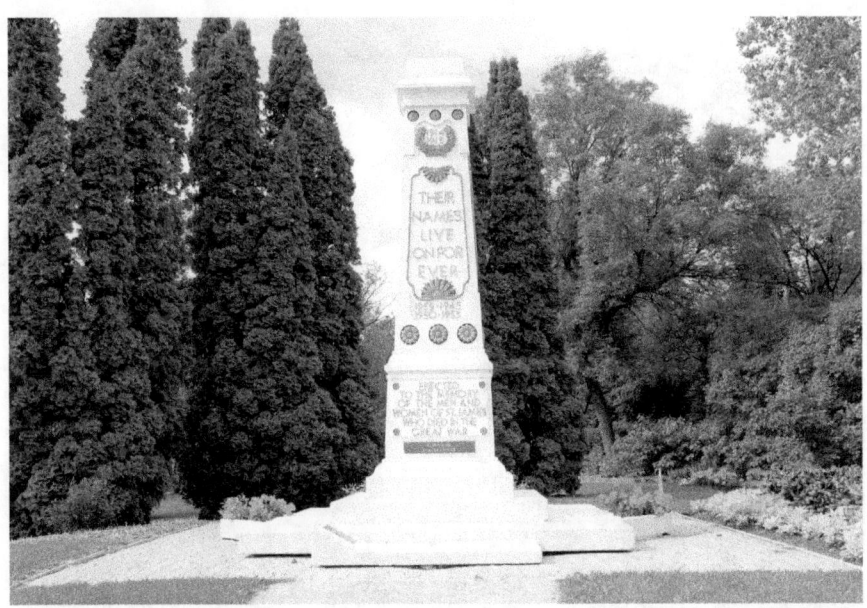

The park is gorgeous and quite popular for cycling, dog walkers, as well as catching frogs in the springs. A Stream from Truro Creek runs through the park, just by the neighbourhood wadding pool. "The Cenotaph was erected in 1936 and pays tribute to fallen soldiers of the First World War. The harsh Winnipeg winters has left the original in poor condition and a second was made to take it's place in 1990 by the St. James Branch of the Royal Canadian Legion. It now honours veterans of the three major wars from the 20th Century."

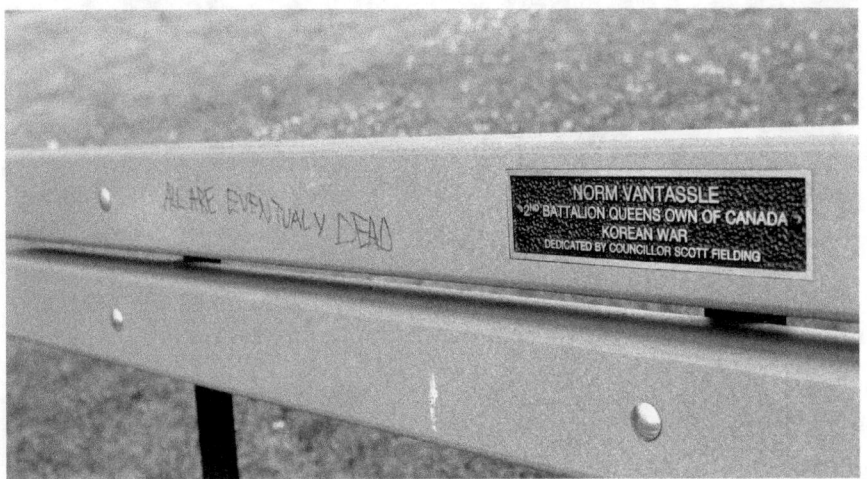

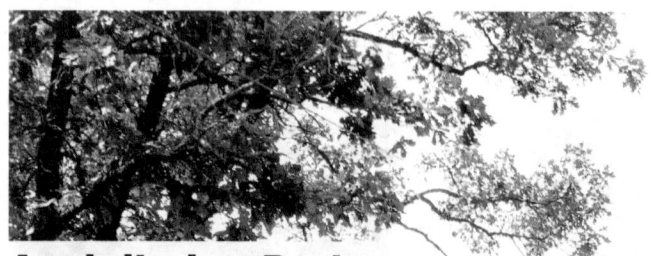

Assiniboine Park

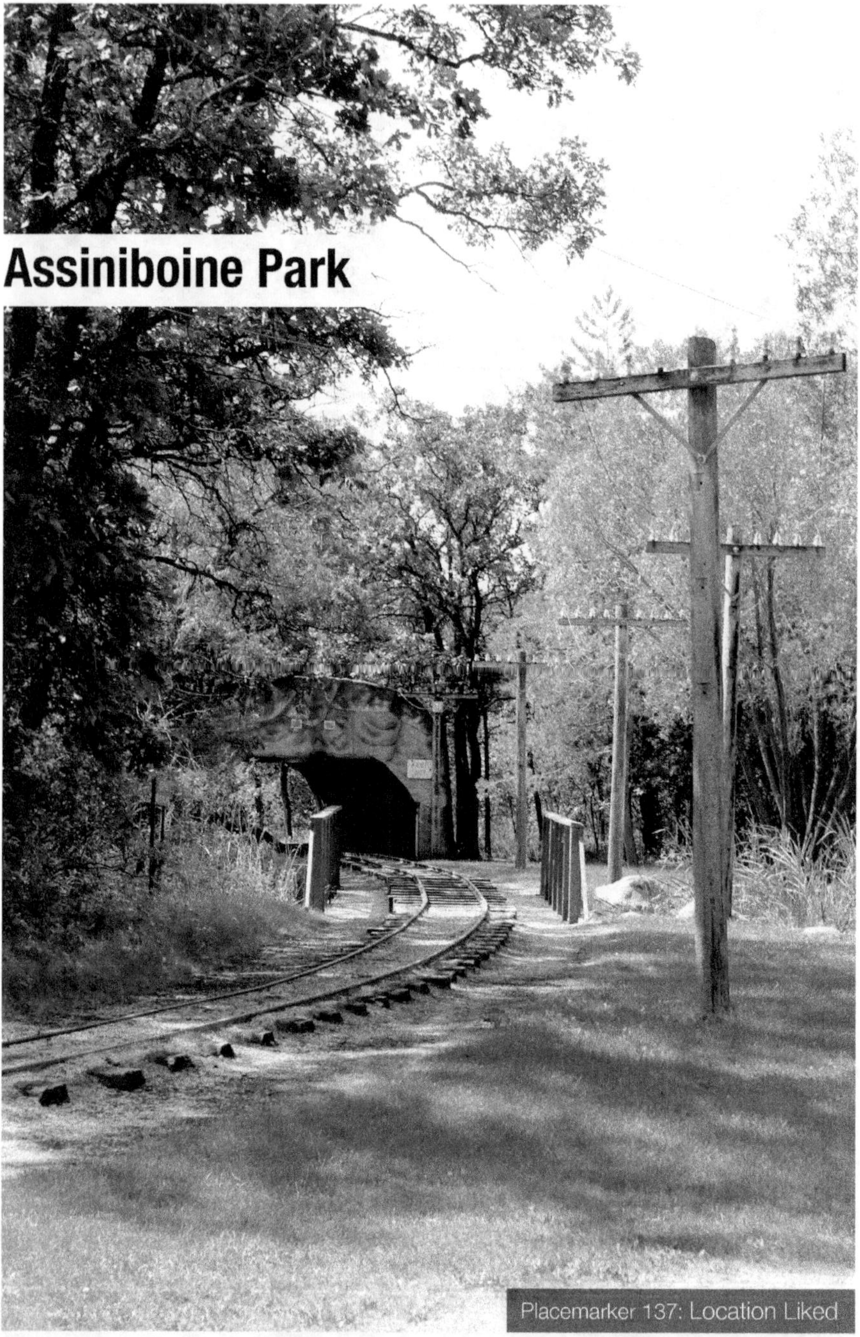

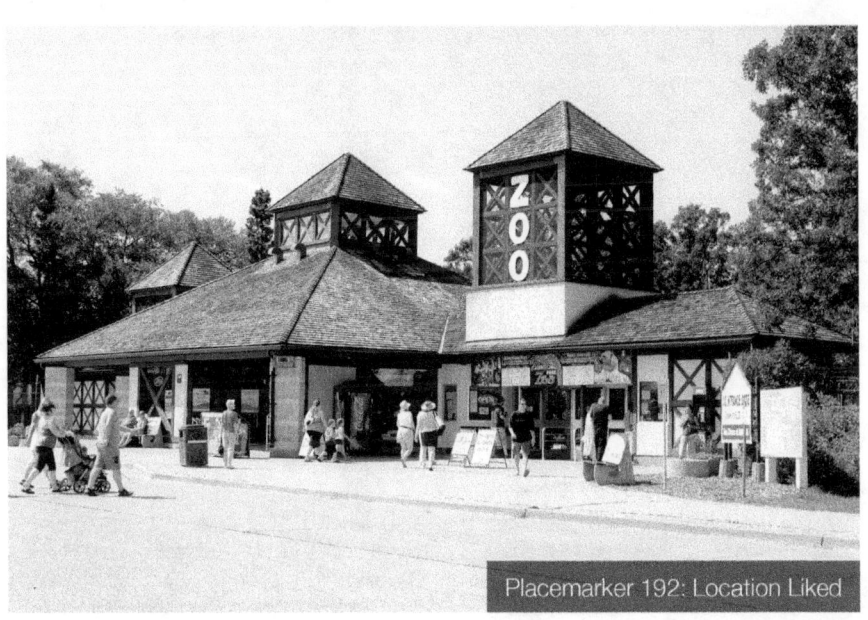

Placemarker 192: Location Liked

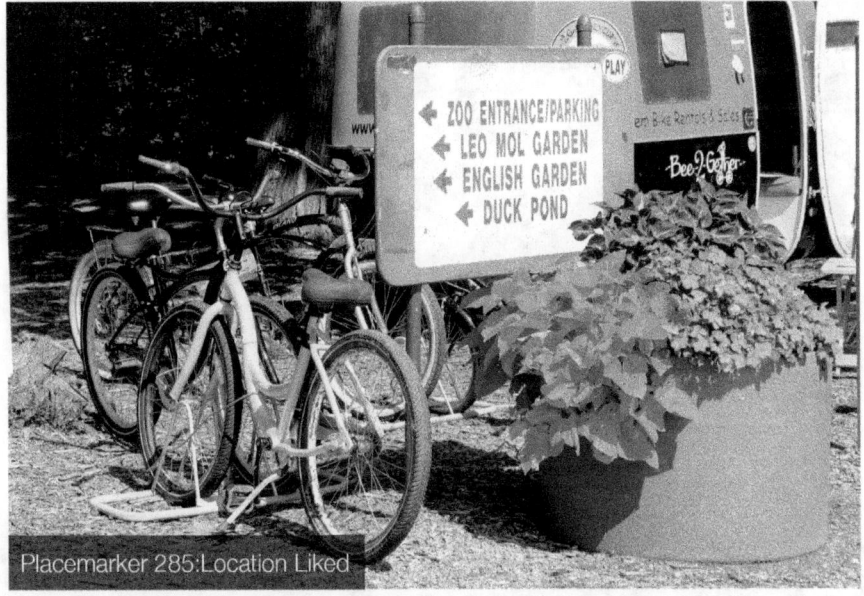

Placemarker 285:Location Liked

Central Park
Placemarker 361 & 84: Ellice Ave. and Edmonton St.

A site under current renovation, but is as lively as ever. The newly installed soccer turf provides the children of the neighbourhood hours of play, while the new play-ground and water park is still gated off. People who live in the many apartment buildings that circle the park, seem to spend more time there than their homes in during the summer days. Families and friends gather, some drinking Slurpees while others have their plastic two litre Stone Cold beer or a bottle Canadian Sherry. On Sundays choir music from Knox United Church trickles from the open doors and into the park.

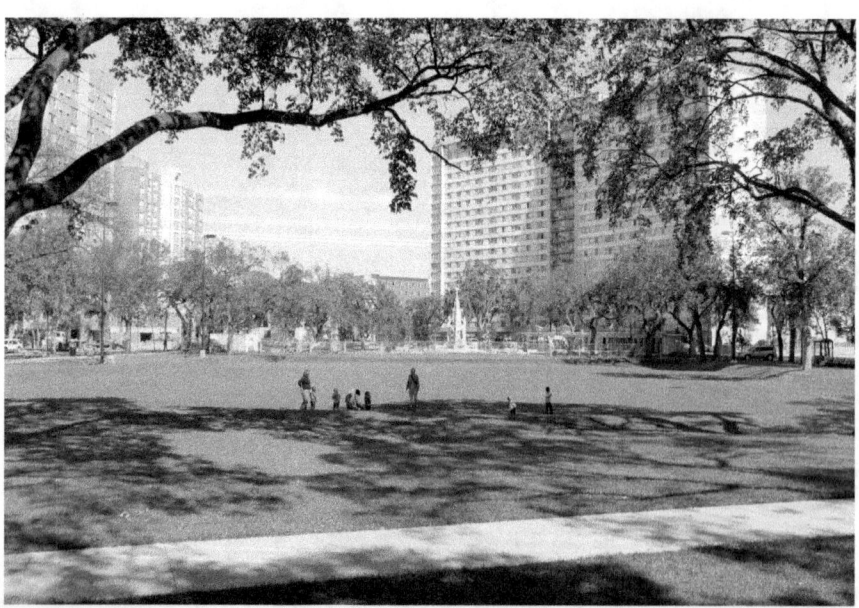

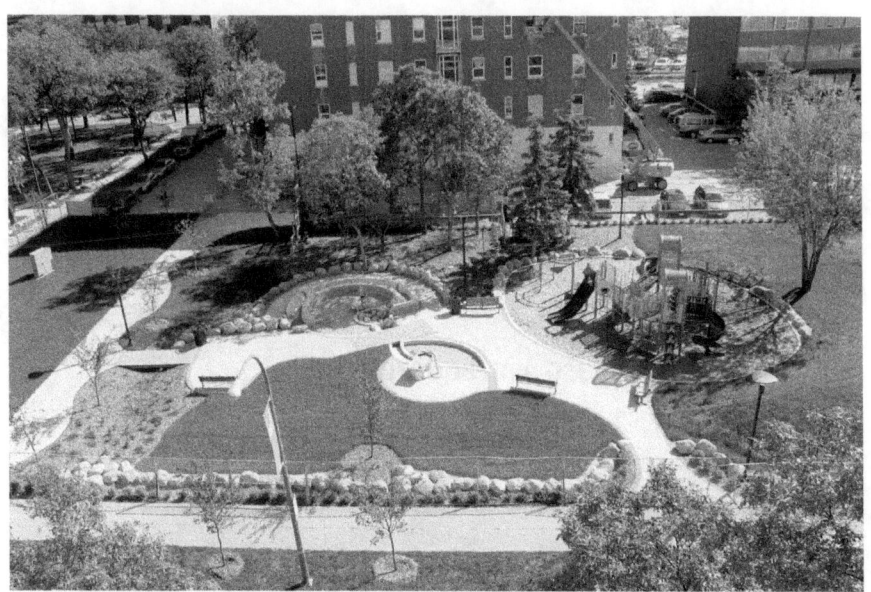

After the church was hit by lightning, their services were occasionally held in the park on summer days. On Fridays locals would turn the park walkway into a market, the loud speakers fill the neighbourhood with songs from the community's respectable motherland. The one element that remains untouched from the original central park, is the Waddel Monumental Fountain which was built in 1913. Thompson explains that the origin of the fountain was based on a challenge set forth by Mr. Wadell's Wife. She would only let him remarry if he built this fountain.

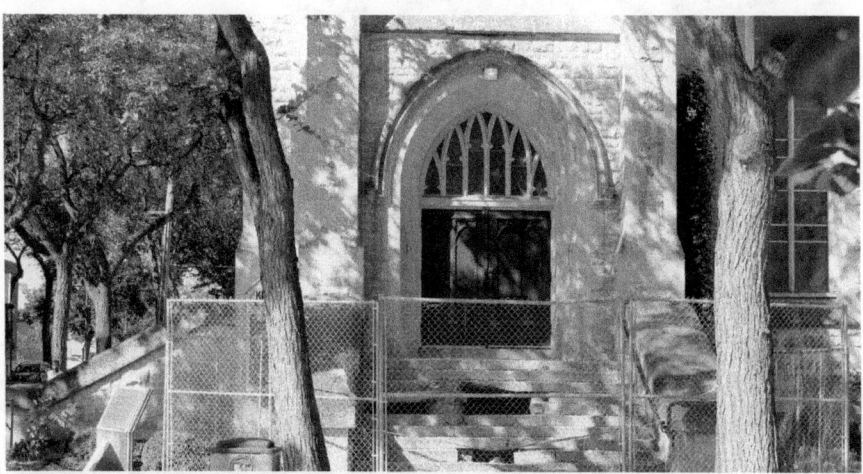

Truro Park
Placemarker 111: Bruce Ave. and Truro St.

This site seemed magical and mysterious during fieldwork. We resorted to online research in hopes to find the origin of this wooded land, sandwiched in between rows
of housing. After an email exchange with a knowledgeable local, we learnt a little bit
more about this site:

"An inventive City employee simply took a bulldozer and made the hill probably in the
late 1950s or 1960s, without permit, invitation or skill. Many of my contemporaries
remember the fun that provided to the neighborhood children. The stone terraces
and stairs were probably a later addition when Gunther Schoch, the city's sole landscape architect, had a look at the bumps and tried to make something of them. We
could never make hills like these in today's rule-ridden environment."

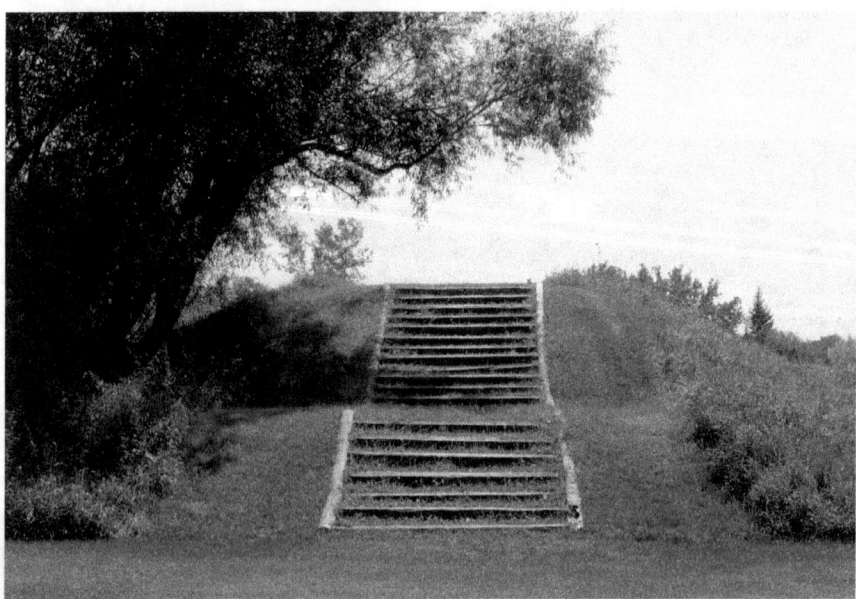

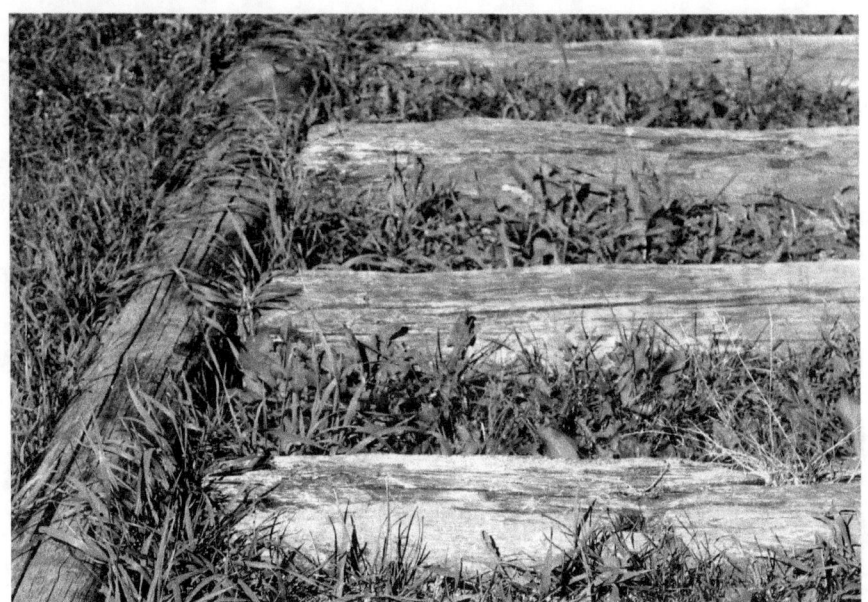

"The most charming use of the park I have seen is as follows:
A woman and her two small children appeared late one morning, rolled out a long sheet of plastic from the top of the slope to the creek, set a hose at the top end and then used this as a chute to fly down the slope.
She told us that her husband was a painter and that's where the plastic came from, and that going to the water slide at Lockport was too expensive and too far to get to."

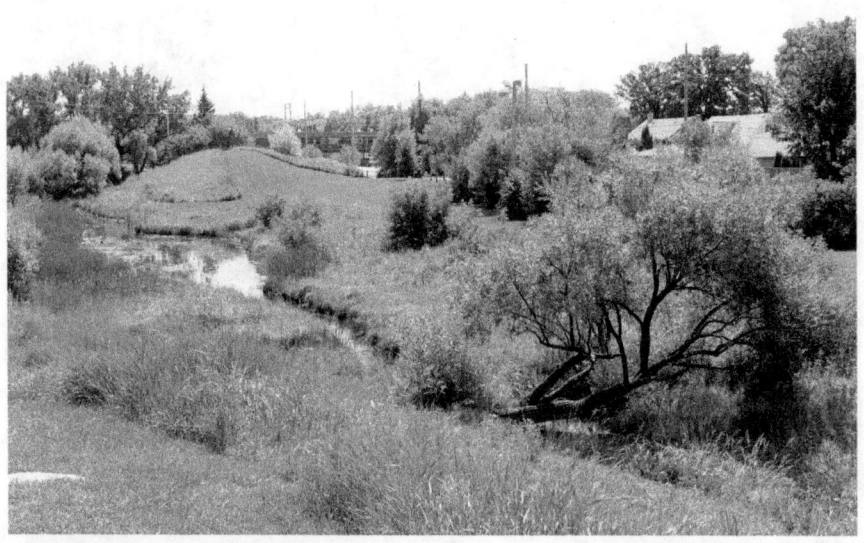

Tuxedo Business Park
Placemarker 92/159/160: Commerce Dr. and Nature Park Way

The newer development of the Tuxedo Business Park still seems to be a work in progress. The landscaped ponds, fountains and lawns, give the area a polished professional demeanour. Flocks of Canadian geese use these artificial ponds as their summer homes. The back of the park is still in development, there are just roads that stop dead with gravel and the remainder of the forest that still has yet to be cut down.

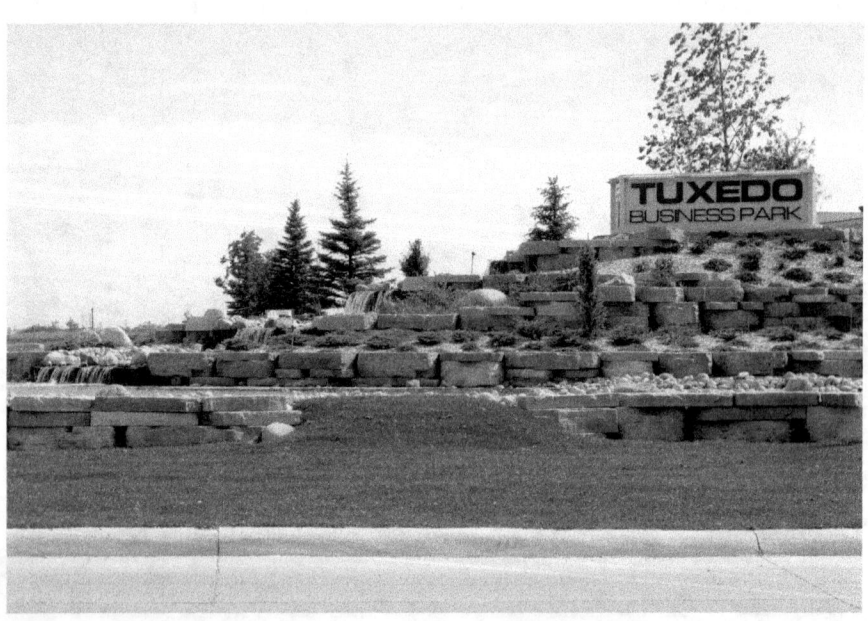

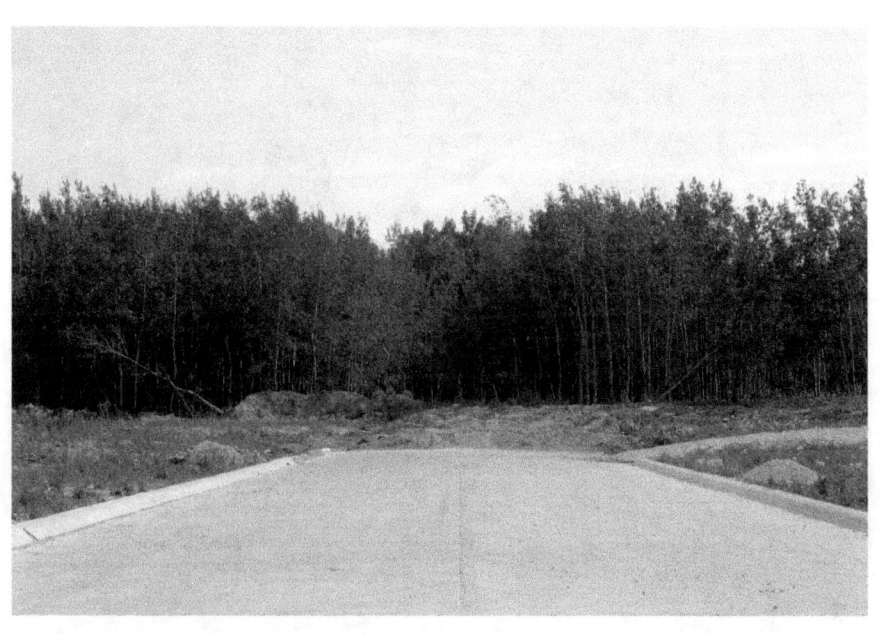

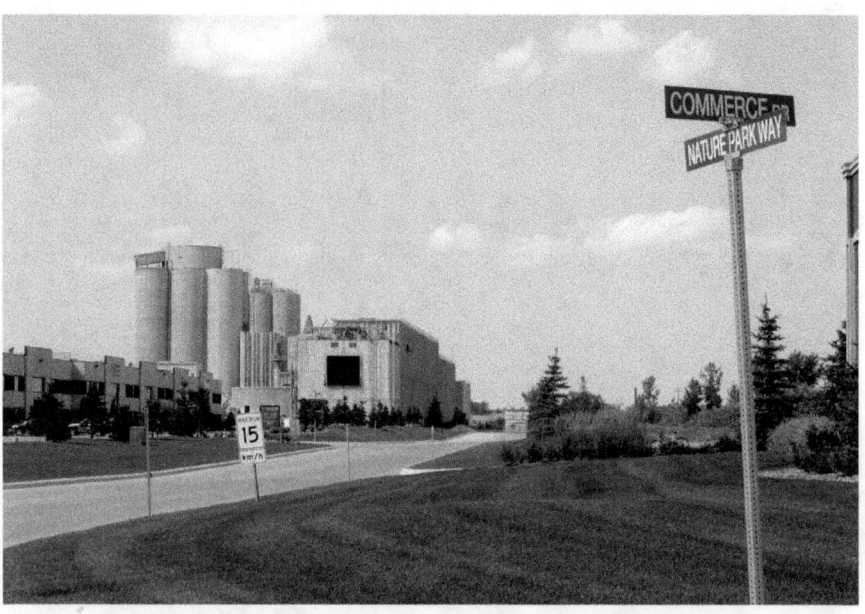

Transformers

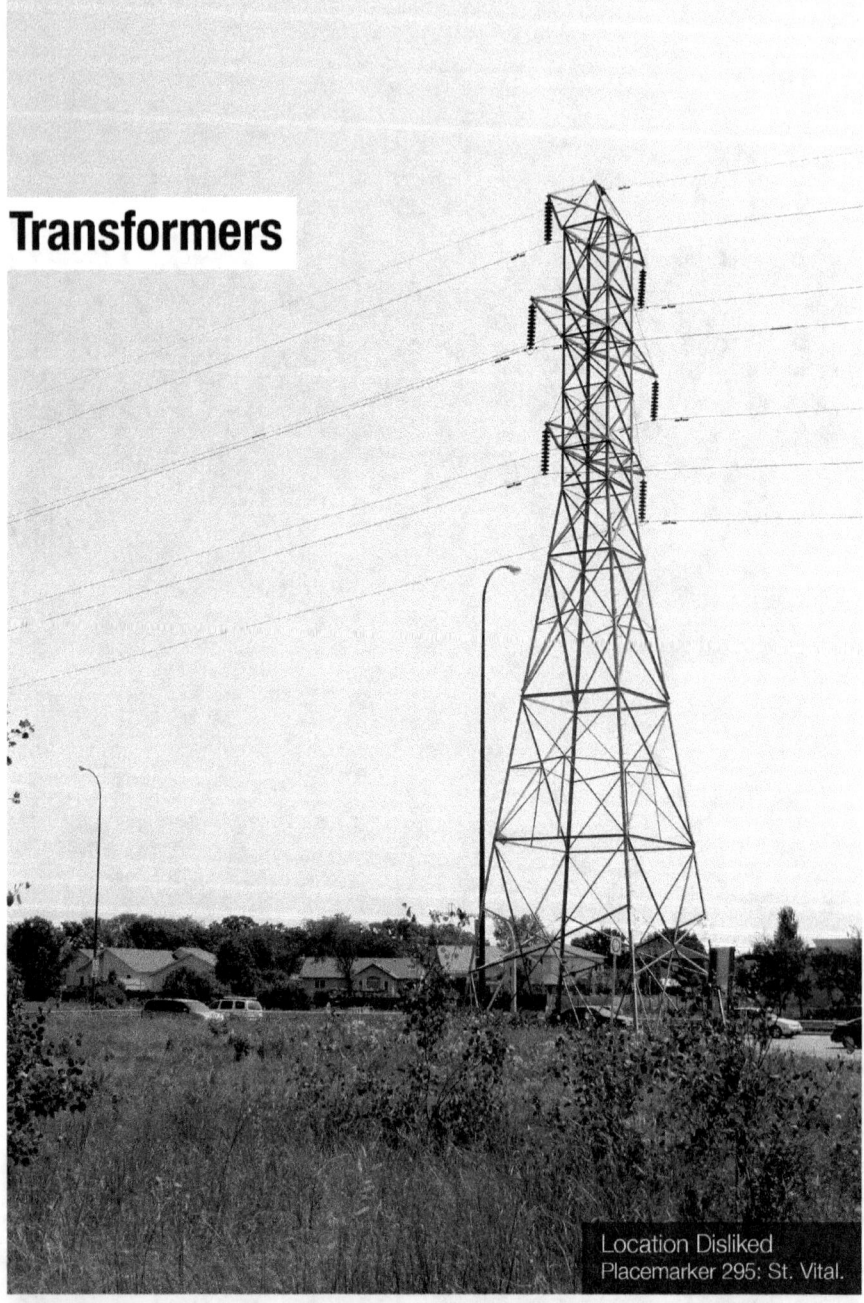

Location Disliked
Placemarker 295: St. Vital.

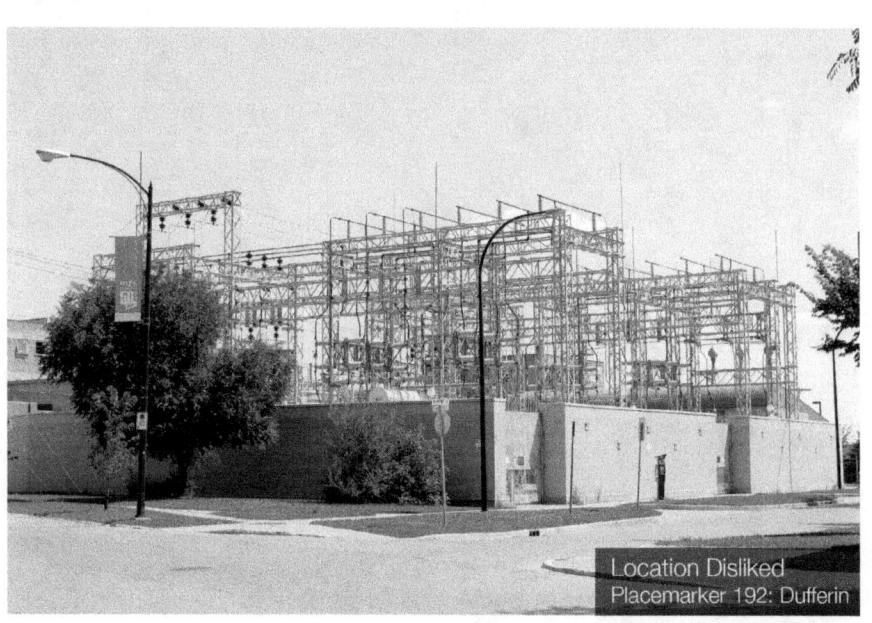

Location Disliked
Placemarker 192: Dufferin

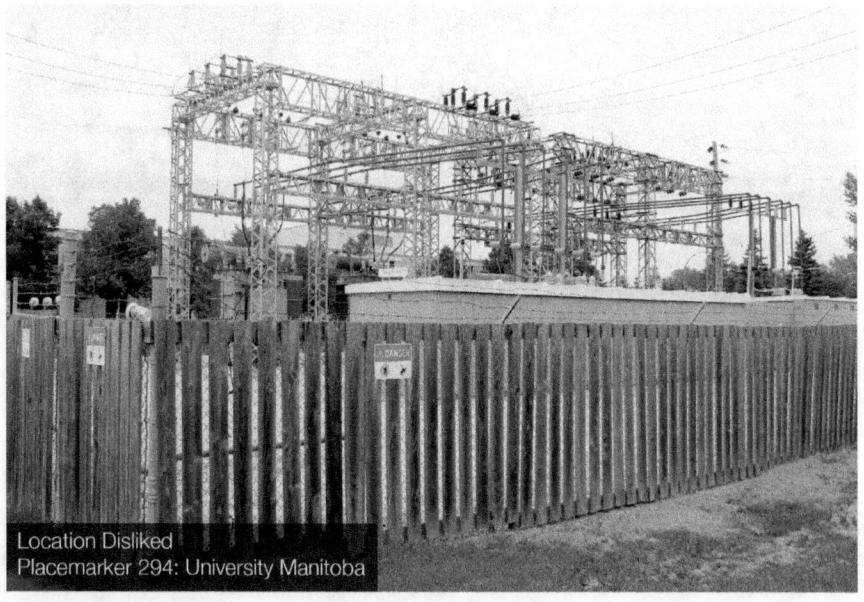

Location Disliked
Placemarker 294: University Manitoba

St Vital Cemetery and Park
Placemarker 222, 225: Near River Rd and Bishop Grandin Blvd

After riding alongside of the Pembina expressway, along the bike path, there is a
small trail is made under an electric transformer. Through the tree and along the river
is a small cemetery with discrete tombstones and benches at opposite sides. No
large signs or markers indicate the name of the cemetery, but it is just off from St.
Vital Park.

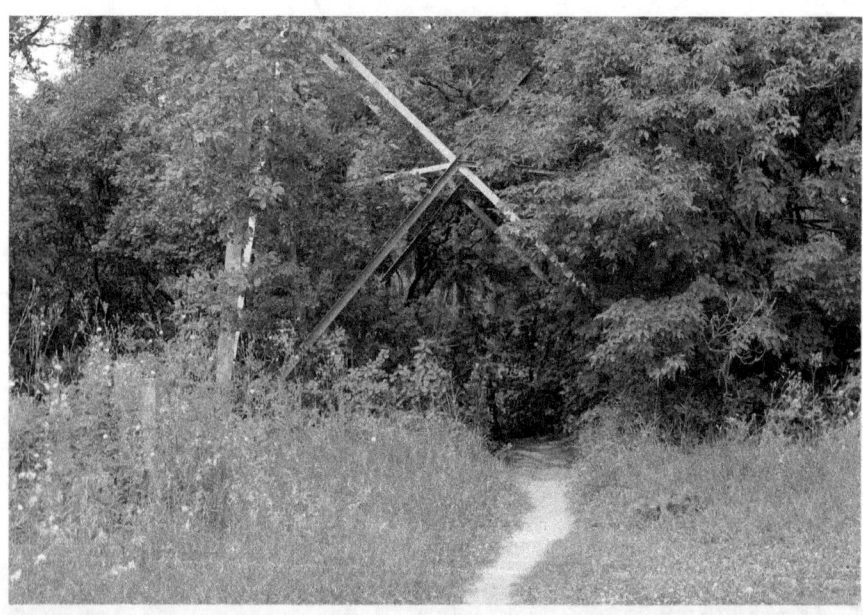

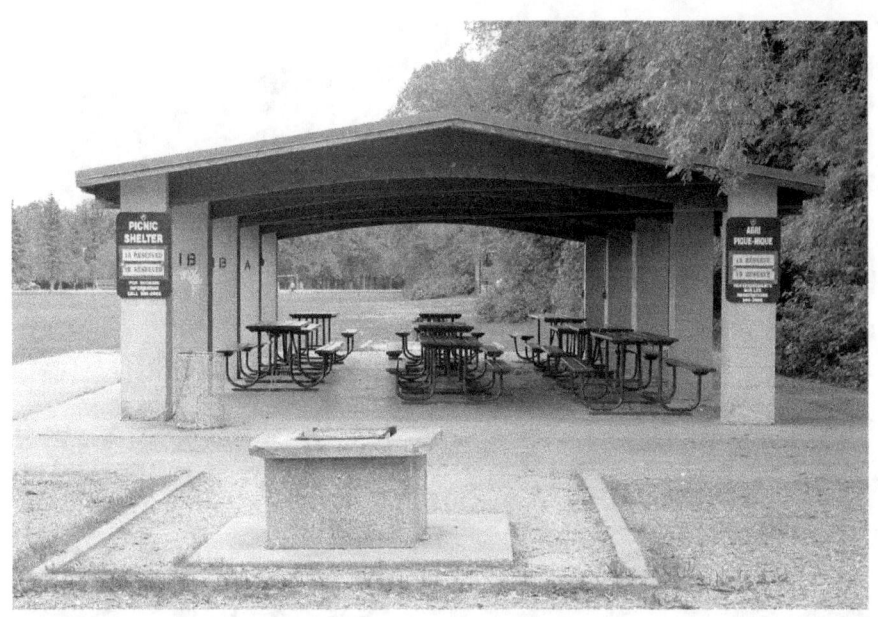

Continuing along the trail leads us to a picnic shelter with a fire pit in which families can book and reserve for the weekend. This hidden trail leads us away from the expressway to family visitors and St. Vital Park.

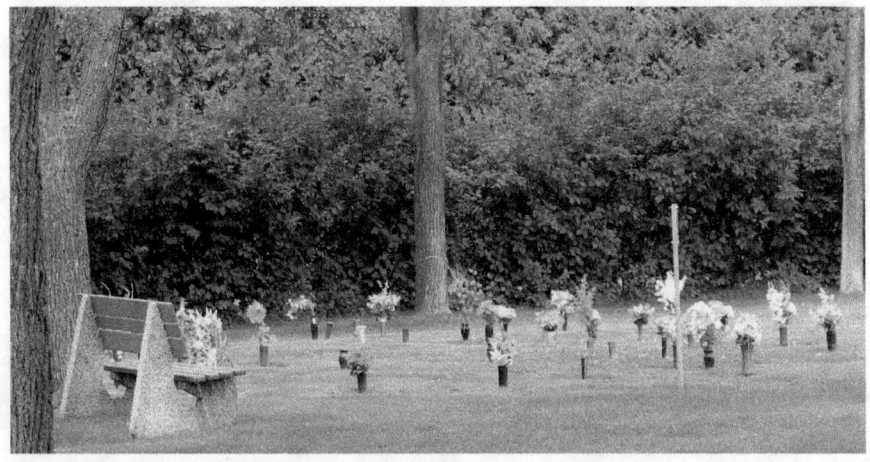

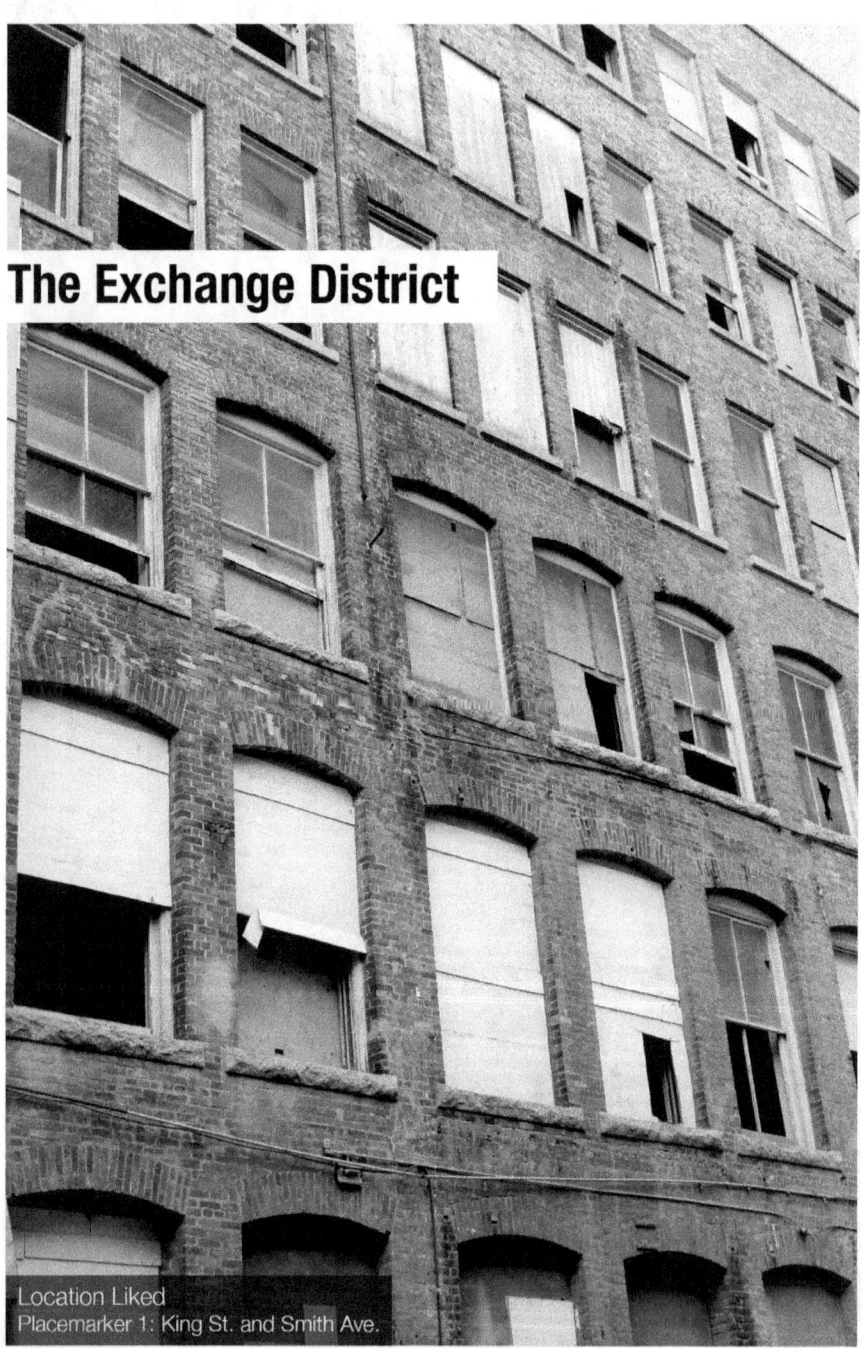

The Exchange District

Location Liked
Placemarker 1: King St. and Smith Ave.

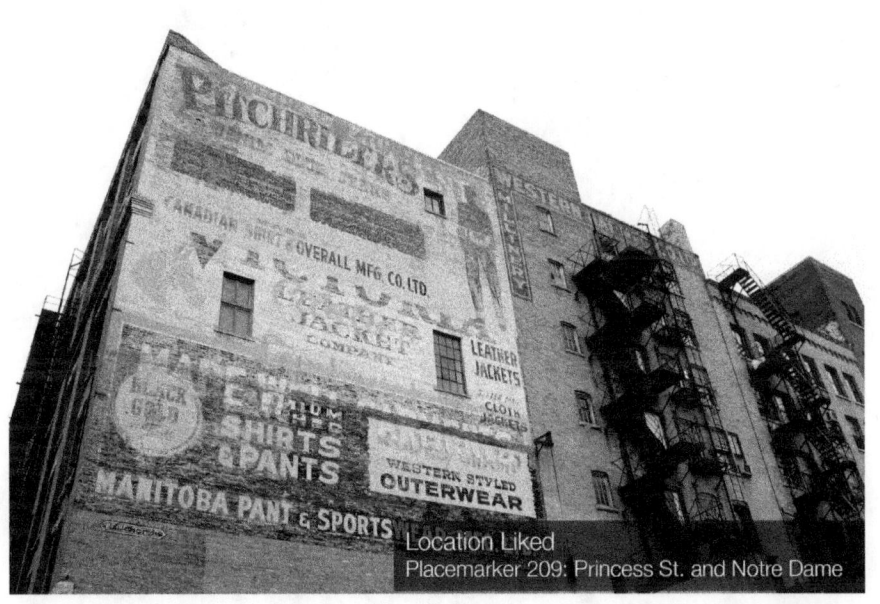

Location Liked
Placemarker 209: Princess St. and Notre Dame

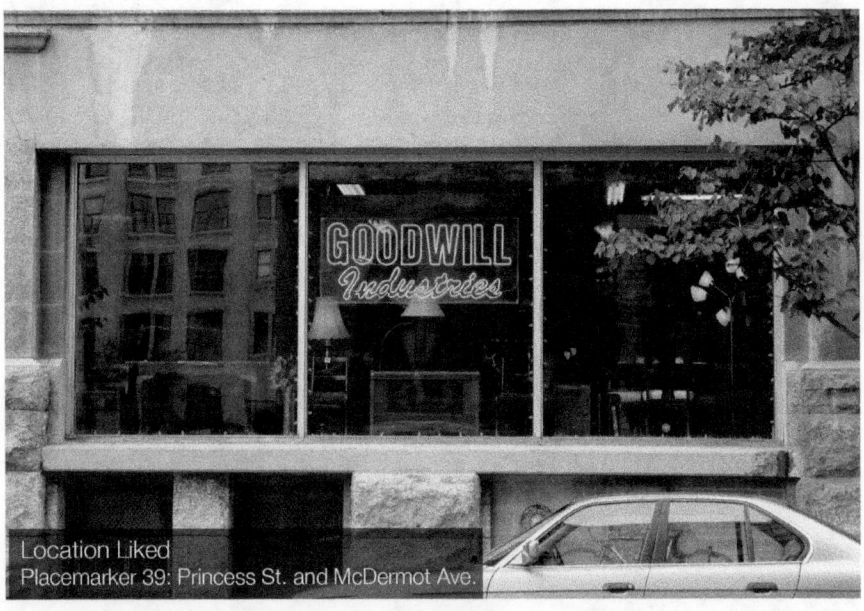

Location Liked
Placemarker 39: Princess St. and McDermot Ave.

70 Arthur from Warehouse to Offices
Placemarker 35 and 139: Albert St. and McDermot Ave

70 Arthur, also known as the Whitla Building is situated in the core of The Exchange District. This building is the home base for many creative-minded businesses and organizations. Formerly a warehouse built with "the influence of the so-called 'first Chicago School' of architects." (Thompson P.23) The building is now divided into office spaces and offices, the wooden floors and aluminum textured ceiling are subtle reminders of aesthetics of the past.

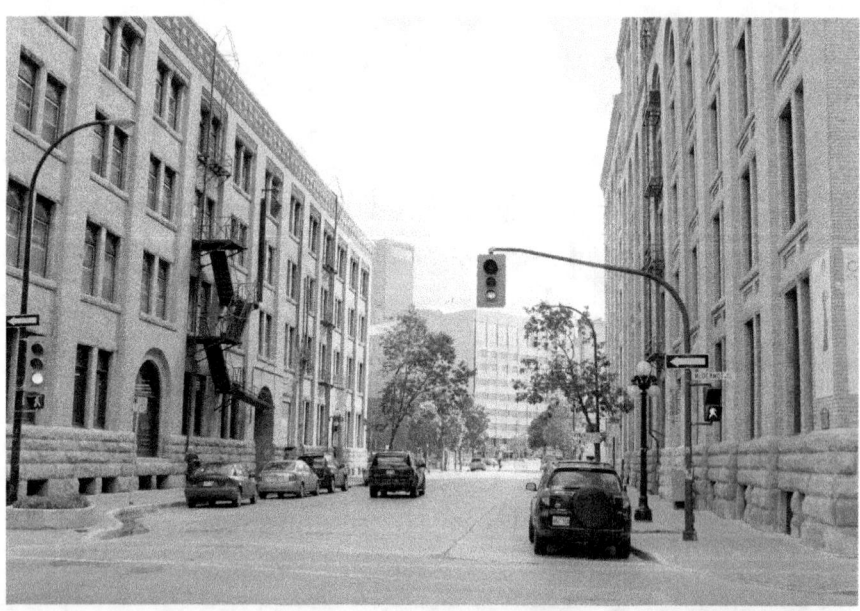

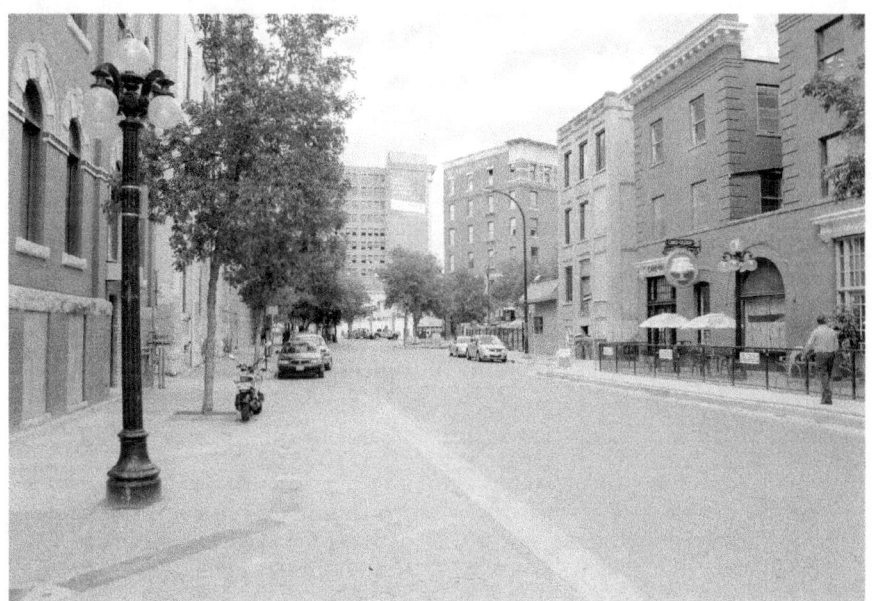

The basement of the building is now converted into The Underground Cafe. Attracting not only the offices above, but the rest of the exchange district, with their one of a kind Fabulous Sun Burger. This building has successfully evolved from a warehouse to an office space that reflects the unique, diverse and creative workforce that The Exchange is notable for.

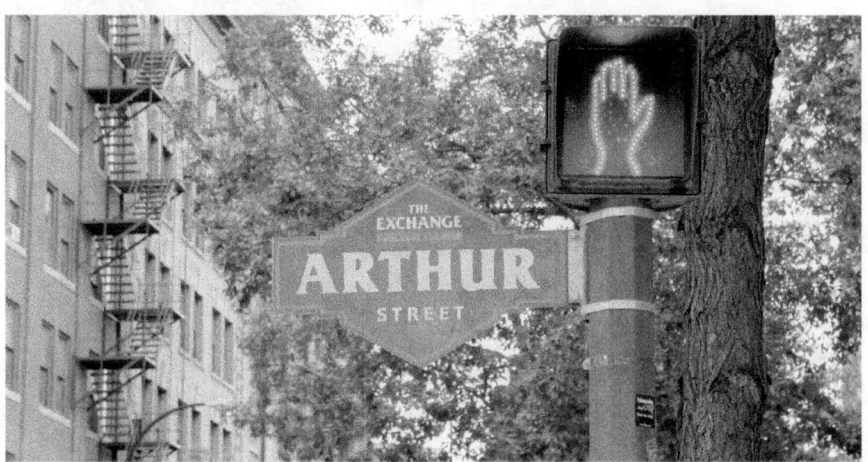

Royal Bank in the Exchange District
Placemarker 359: Main St. and William Ave.

The Royal bank in the Exchange District seemed that it was in a state of transition. But to the people of Winnipeg the site held memories from their teenage years. The building was more than just a bank, as stories of secret late night escapades came to the surface.

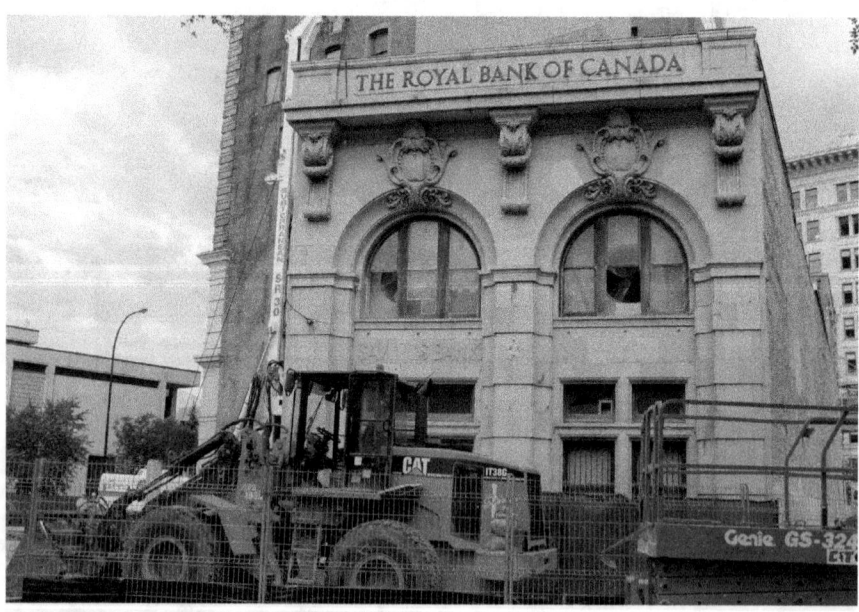

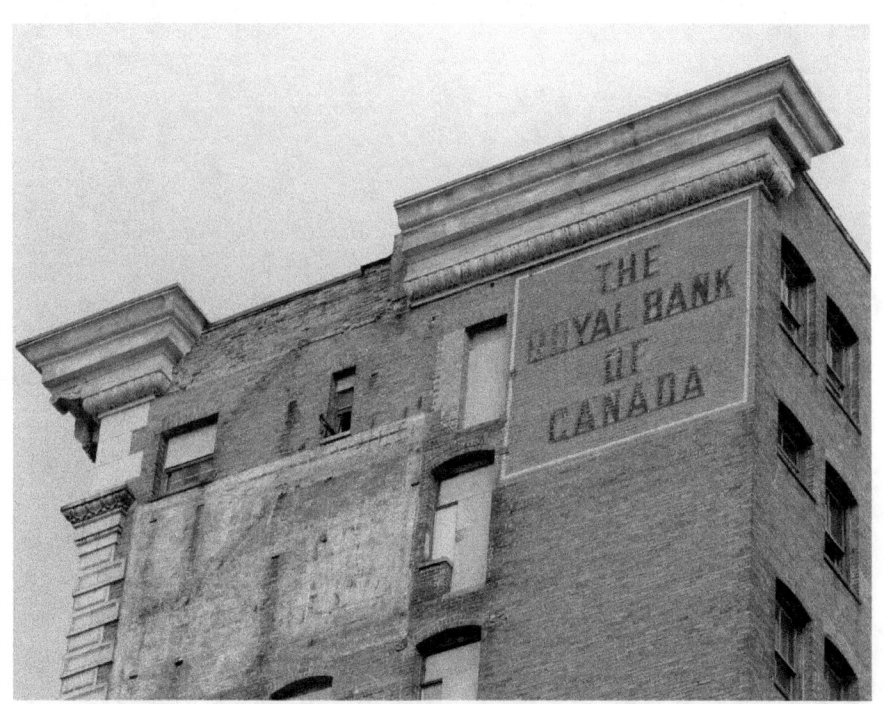

Please choose a dot on the map or a photo on the wall and tell us what you think of it.

Location: The Royal Bank Building.

Liked/Disliked: A large group of us used to break in all the time & have massive parties

Why: throughout the building kaja including on top of the roof.

The 1919 Winnipeg Strike Mural
Placemarker 256: Main St. behind Whisky Dixs

Standing in the parking lot behind Whisky Dixs, one can see this mural painted by Tom Andrich in 2006. This piece was a part of Mural Fest 2K6, the image illustrates the 1919 Winnipeg Stike.

> "I chose the 1919 Winnipeg Strike as a Mural project because the Strike was of great importance to Winnipeg's history and to the Labour movement in Canada. The present generation knows little about the strike. A Mural is an excellent way to bring history into the present –to educate and to promote discussion. I've attempted to depict the anger, the confusion, the violence, the passion, and the hugeness of the event. Over 30,000 people out of a city of 200,000 participated in the strike. Individuals gave up their freedom and went to jail to advance the cause. People from all types of employment and from all walks of life were united- even the police force went on strike!! Thugs were hired by the city to replace the police!!" - Tom Andrich (Winnipeg Murals)

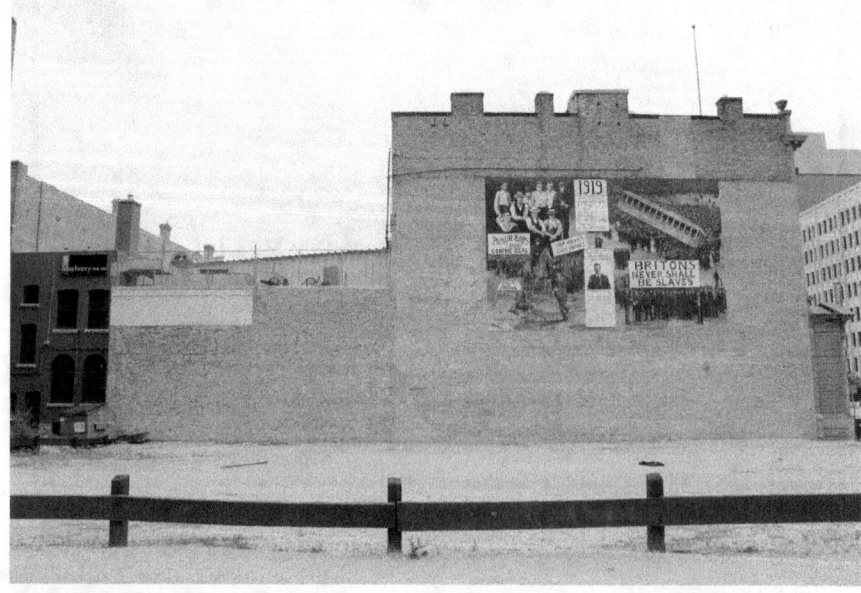

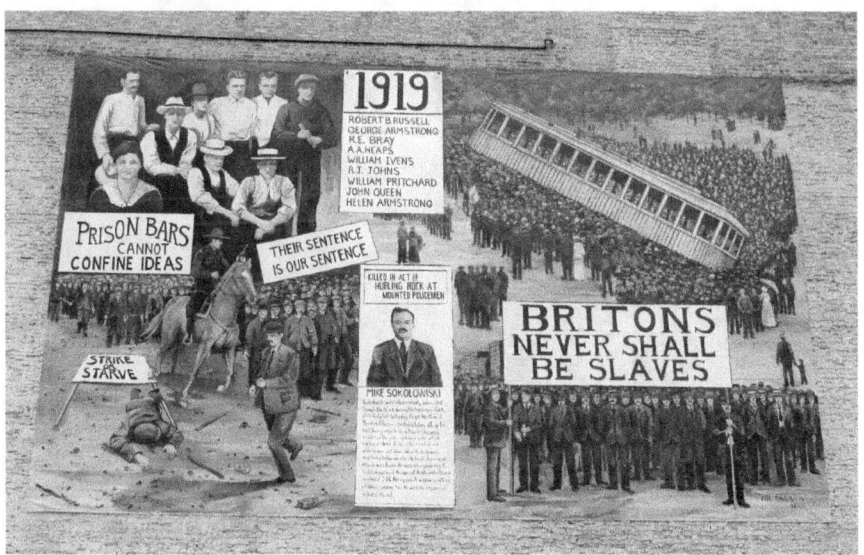

Winnipeg Murals explains that the mural depicts the rioting that underwent that day where a crowd of strikers overturned a streetcar in front of city hall on Bloody Saturday. June 21st marked the day where the Federal Government decided to stop the strike by sending in the Royal Northwest Mounted Police, leaving over a hundred injured and the death of Mike Sokolowiski. The officials did not want to point fingers on the strikers who were actually jobless soldiers returning to war, so they blamed the foreigners (strikers of British background) In the top left corner is an image of the eight main leaders who lead the strike, including Mrs. Helen Armstrong a woman who was sent to prison several times.

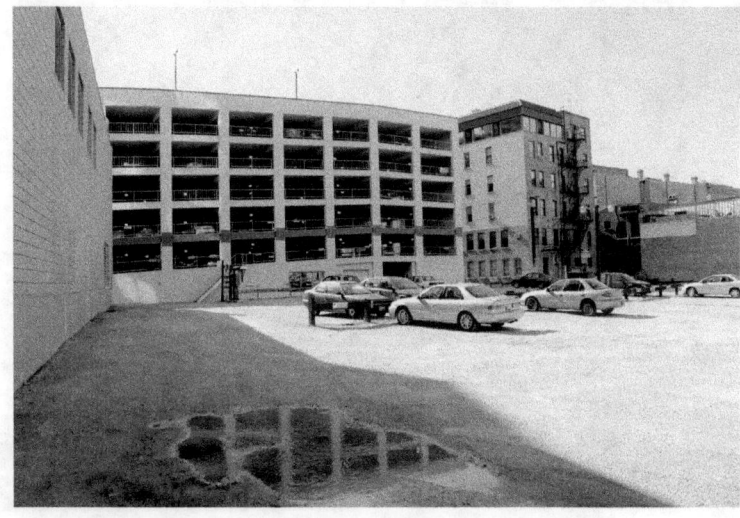

North Point Douglas

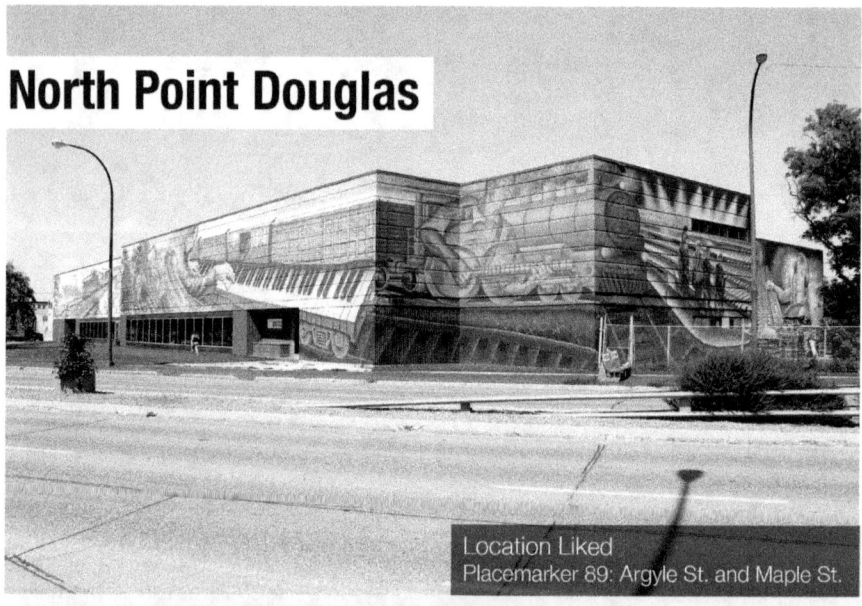

Location Liked
Placemarker 89: Argyle St. and Maple St.

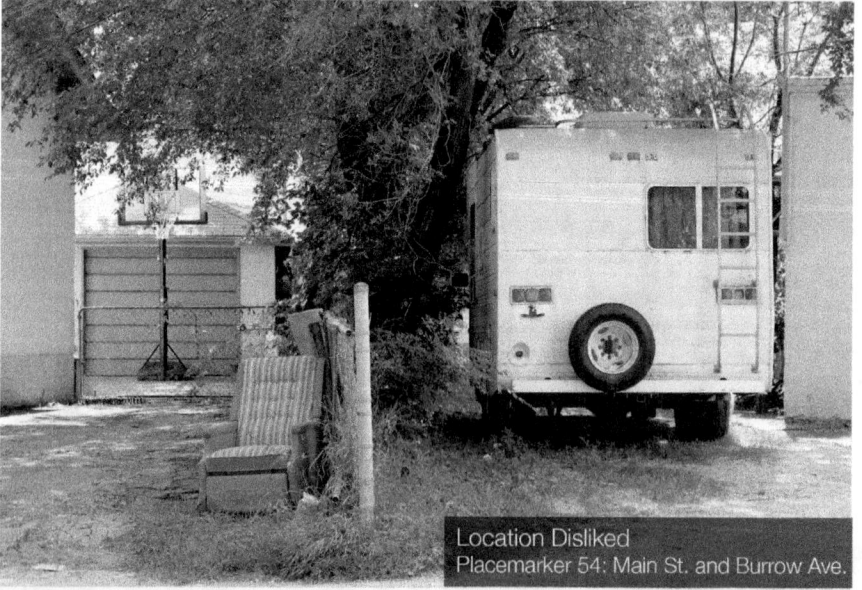

Location Disliked
Placemarker 54: Main St. and Burrow Ave.

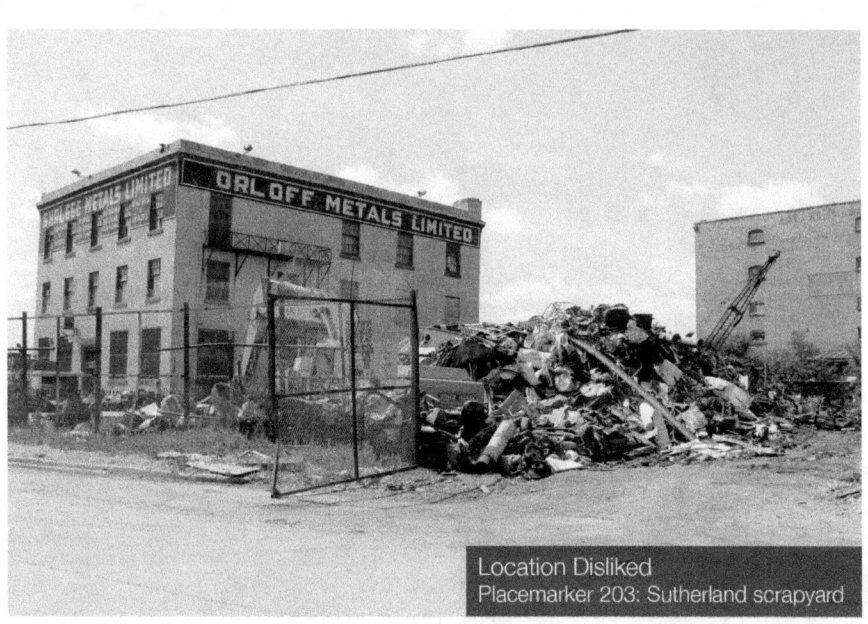

Location Disliked
Placemarker 203: Sutherland scrapyard

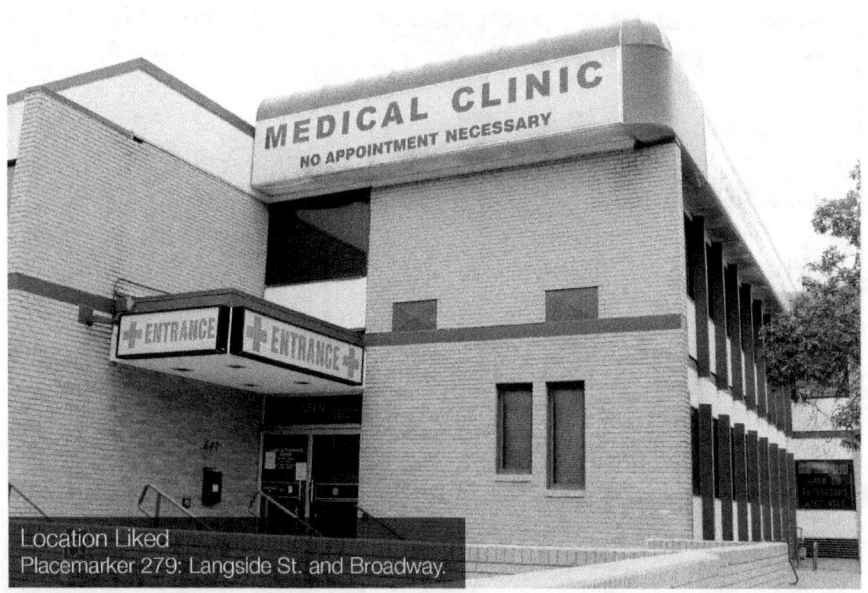

Location Liked
Placemarker 279: Langside St. and Broadway.

Holy Trinity Ukrainian Orthodox Cathedral
Placemarker 350/73: Main St. and College Ave

This cathedral was picked as both a liked and disliked site. It is a positive site because the cathedral structure is overwhelmingly ornate. This sentiment was confirmed by a participant at the Tallest Poppy. One element that could contribute to the site being tagged as a disliked location, is the loud bells that ring multiple times throughout the day. These bells can be heard throughout the surrounding residential areas, and may pose as a problem for homeowners.

Please choose a dot on the map or a photo on the wall and tell us what you think of it.

Location:
Location - CHURCH PHOTO - MAIN St. BESIDE ST. JOHN PARK

Liked/Disliked: *LOVE THE MOSAIC tiles*

Why: *thE DETAIL IS STUNNING!*

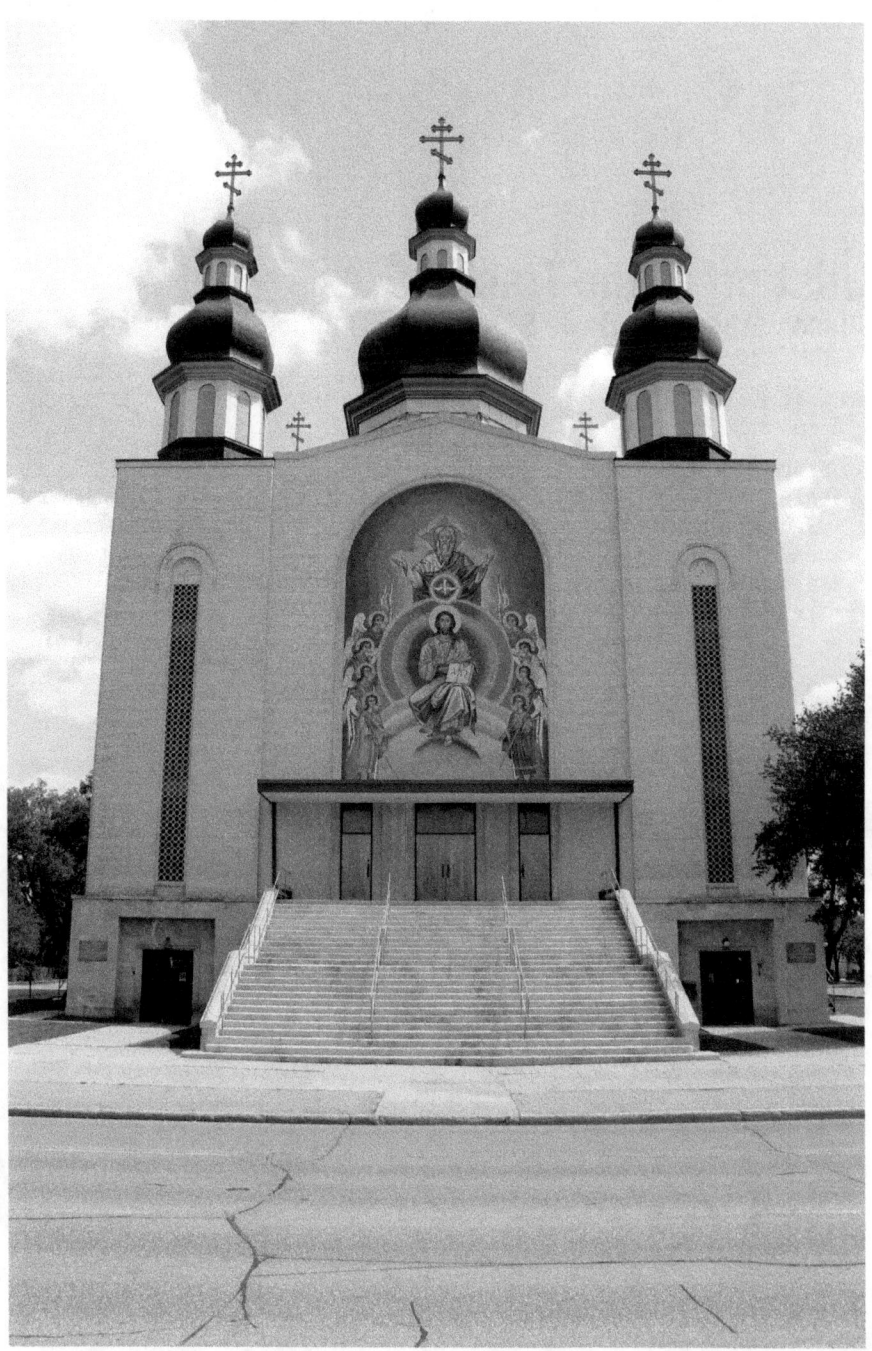

Just off of the Tracks
Placemarker 145: Boyle St and Point Douglas Ave

Scattered along Point Douglas road are large rusted metal containers that once held water and grain. Near by in the grassy fields are large deserted machines that were once used for either farming or mining nearby. At the end of the road there is a large old hand painted sign attached to a barbed wire fence that reads "No Smoking or Parking on Gateway Property." To the left of the road is a poorly boarded up building with an old rental sign covered by untrimmed bushes.

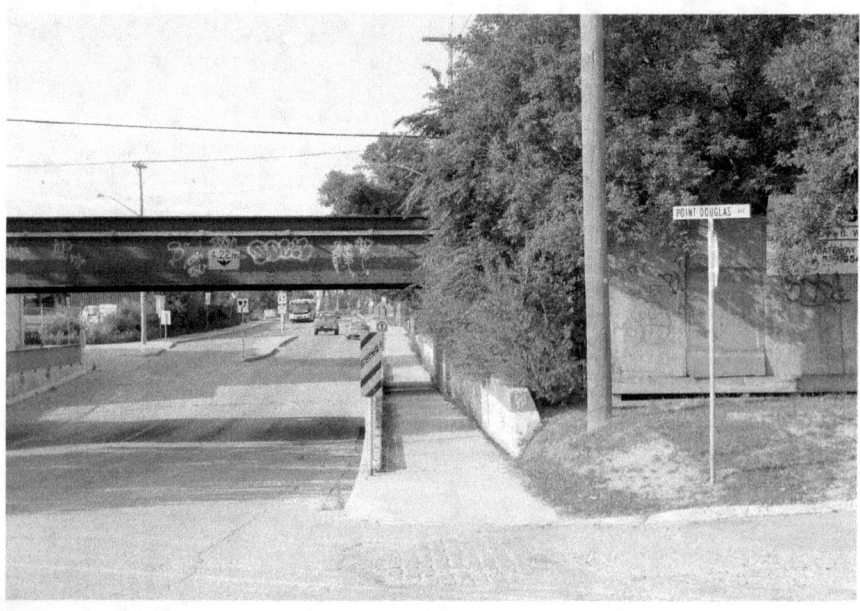

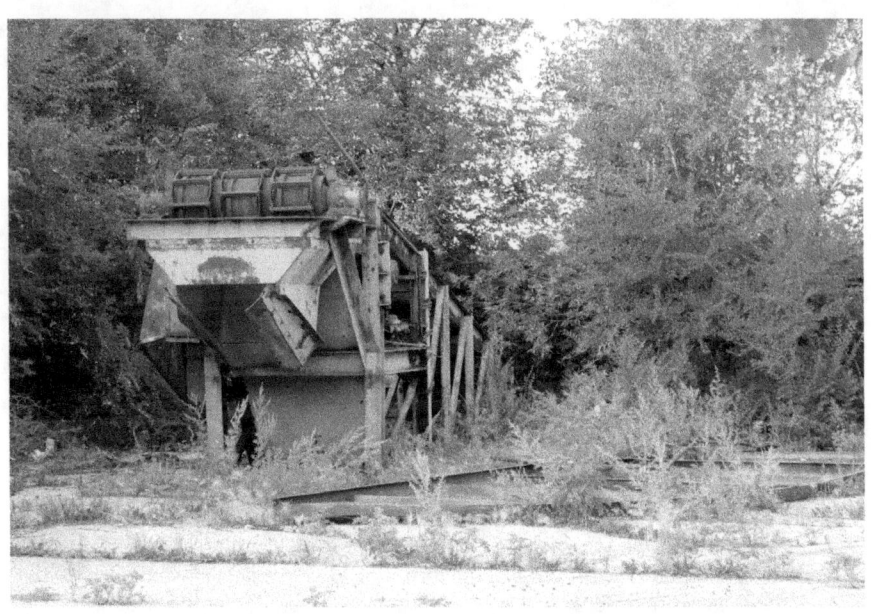

The site is ideal for graffiti culture to exist due to the lack of traffic and these alley be-tween vacant and abandoned buildings. It is overwhelming to be standing in the tall grassy meadows with these large industrial machines scattered in pieces. The road leads to a small residential district with a group of houses that seem to match this area with structures that are just as dilapidated as the equipment is.

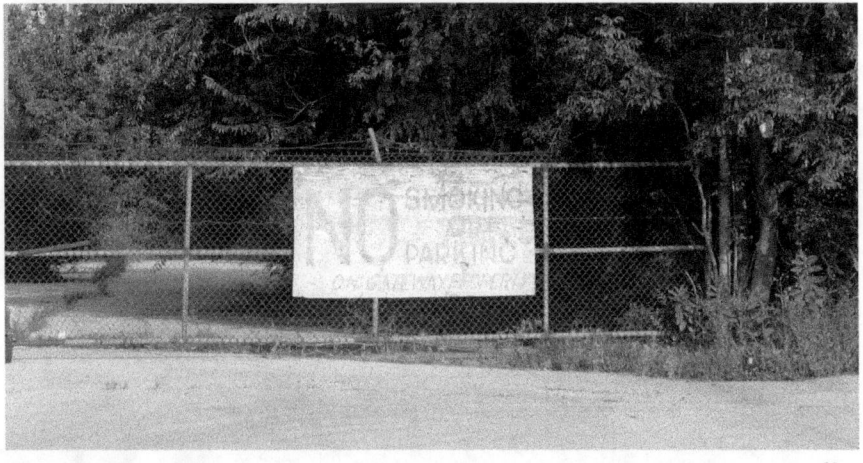

Junkyard & Someone's Home
Placemarker 390: Edge of Point Douglas Park

At the far edge of Point Douglas Park, past the wooded perimeter, sits a clearing. A variety of metal objects are haphazardly collected and rusting. A truck container with the door ajar is clustered next to a trailer and two large cylindrical storage units. Two mangled silos, sit in the foreground acting as a barrier to the rest of the clearing. One silo gaped open at the top, creates a cave like hollow. It was clear that this was someone's home.

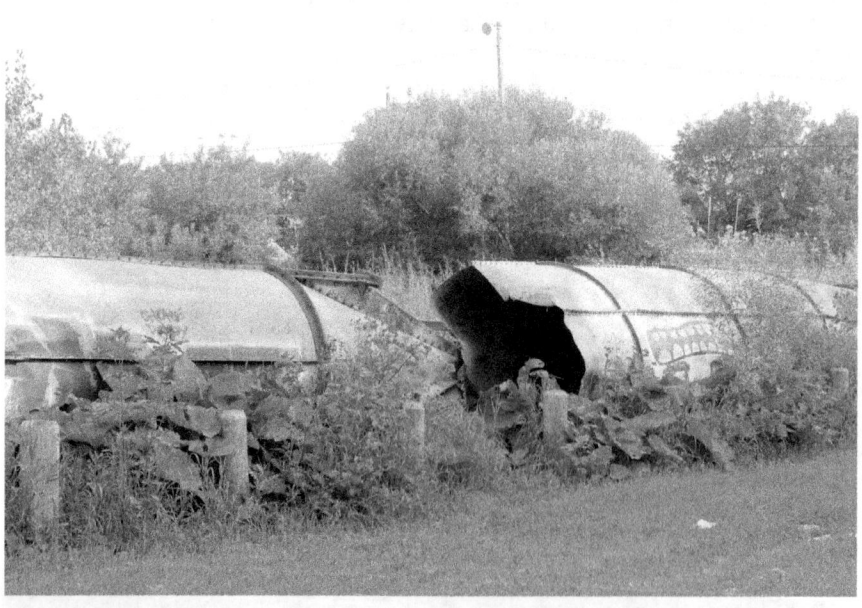

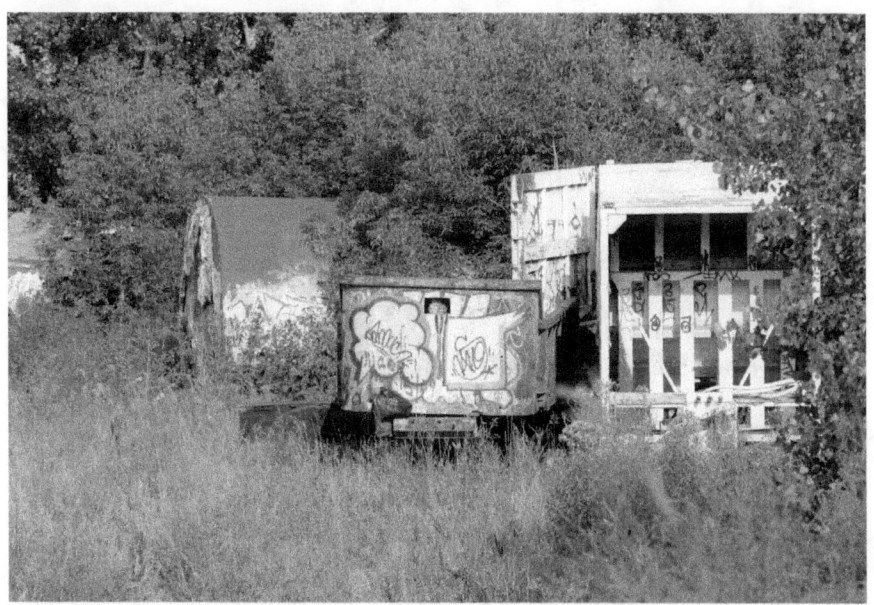

Magazines spilled out on to the grass. An uneasy air rests over the tattered remains, leaving an individual with a myriad of questions running through their minds about what was, and what this place has become. They will all remain unanswered because your gut says walk away.

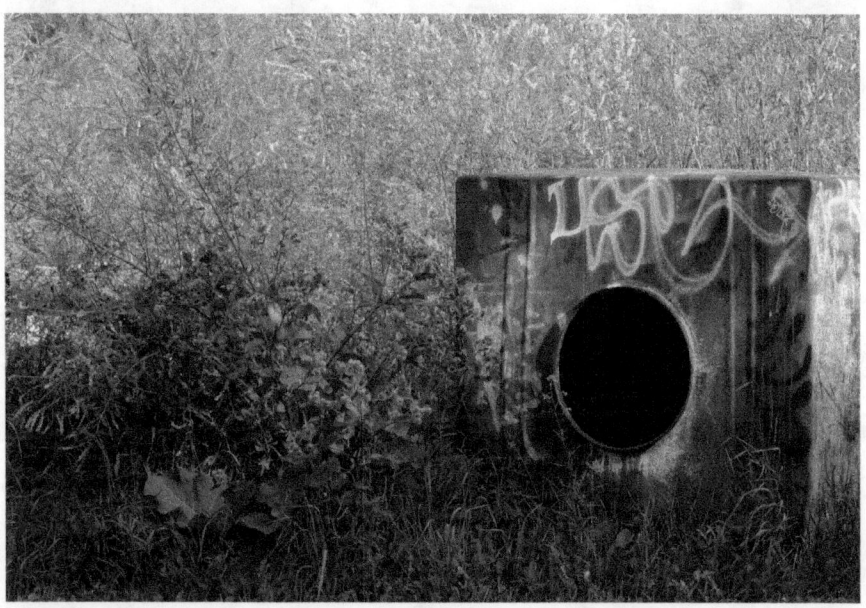

A Love Bridge
Placemarker 88: Osborne St. and Jessie Ave.

This favoured spot is located north on Main street by an underpass below a railway. Situated near an electrical transformer and aside from the busy traffic are murals made by children and artists. The images range from a prairie scene with travellers on horse drawn wagons crossing a field filled with busy farmers, to an imaginative futuristic city with sky trains and tunnels integrated within the landscape of forests and mountains.

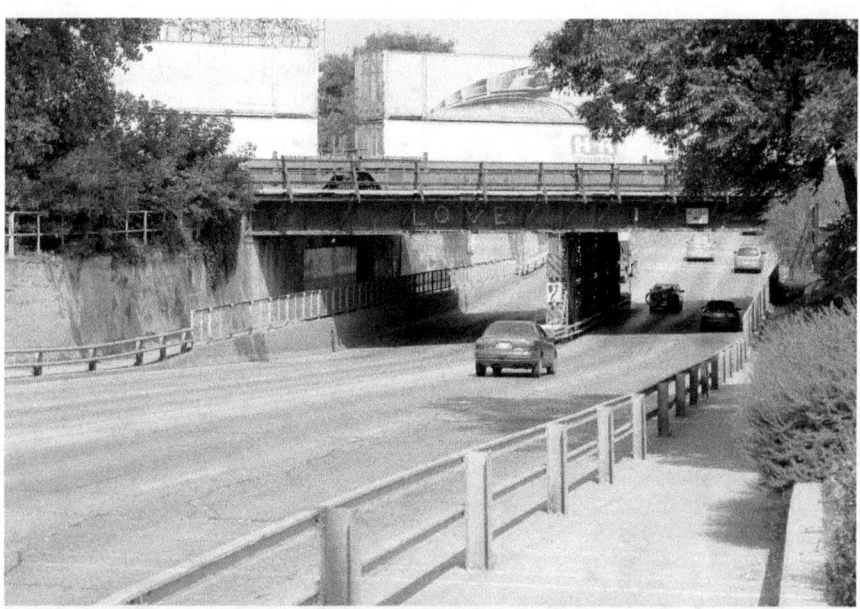

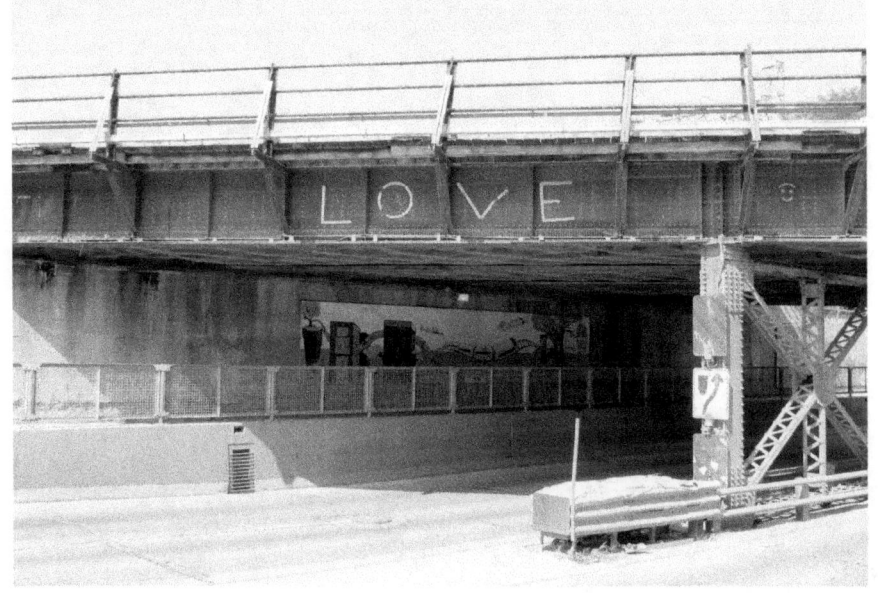

The passage underneath this bridge appears to be an alternative space to display murals within a public space. The word "Love" is written on the overpass, built from numerous circular price tags. The flow of sounds from the train rails and busy cars is constant and prominent, the two cross at this perpendicular intersection never touching and barely aware of the images and stories underneath them.

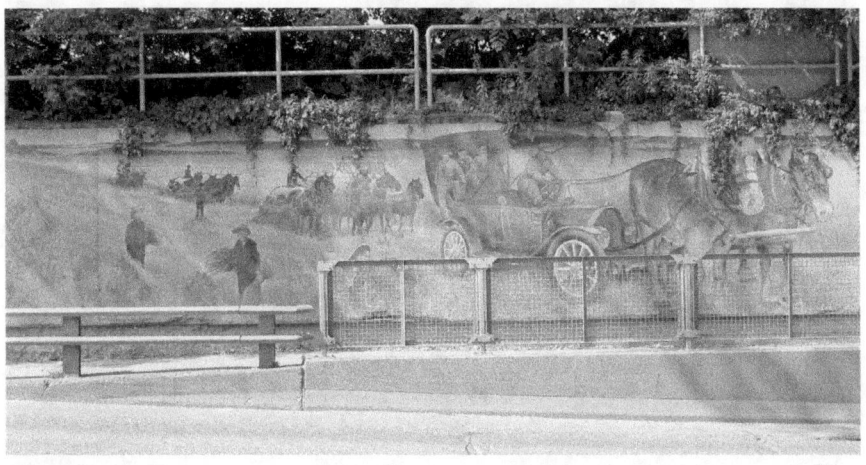

Close by the River
Placemarker 89: At the End of Mulvey Ave and Osborne St.

"No Dumping Violators will be prosecuted under the solid waste by Law - City of Winnipeg" reads the metal sign at the end of a path made from cobble stone by the riverside. Behind the gas stations and garage is a bike path that runs along Osborne village and into this unfavored site.

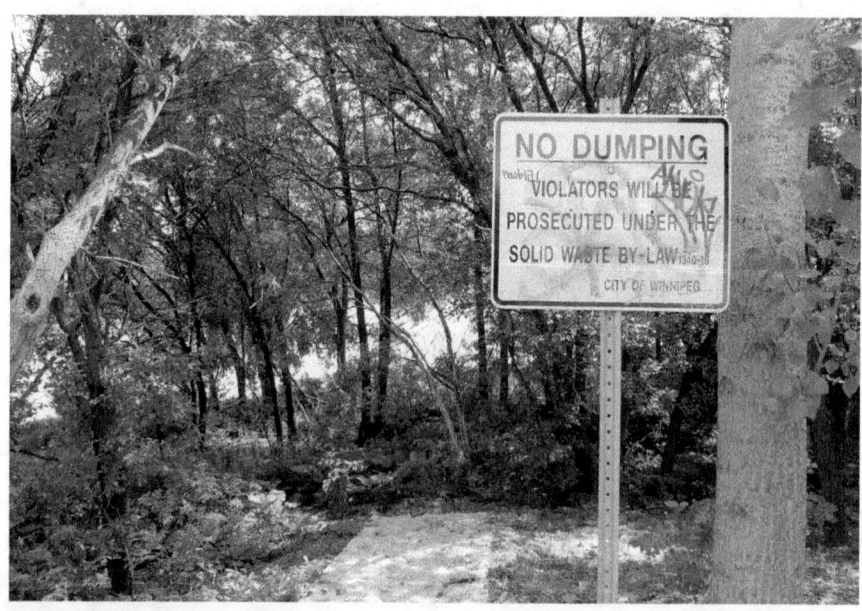

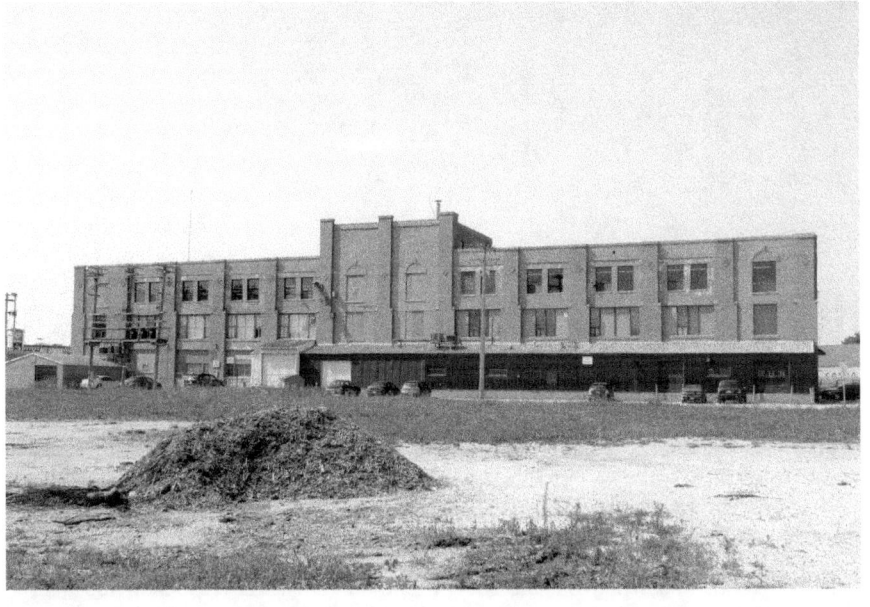

A discarded semi-trailer label "Riverbend Movers" sits still in the lot of "CJ Storage," a large building with a poor splotchy blue paint job and large piles of wood-chips around it. The dandelions and the tall patches of grass are numerous amongst the half-forgotten/non-functional vehicles. Their neighbour is a large industrial building that is currently a shipping plant. Fences and power lines break up the large empty lot, they are parallel with the bike path's beautiful riverside view.

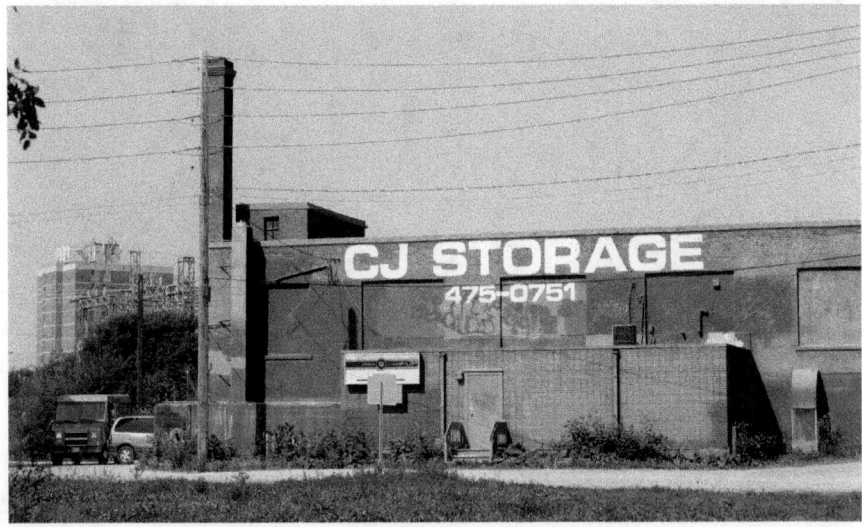

Home Street
Placemarker 23: Home St. and Ellice Ave.

This site seemed to be a more symbolic reference then a liked site. During field research we combed the street up and down looking for a positive site. It was a residential area, and nothing was jumping out at us. Finally, just before giving up, we sat
at the street corner trying to figure out where to go from there. We looked above us
only to realize that the street name was Home Street. We felt that the participates
reference to this site was more of a sentimental love letter to Winnipeg then anything
else. Our suspicions where confirmed when a Tallest Poppy participant wrote about
this site.

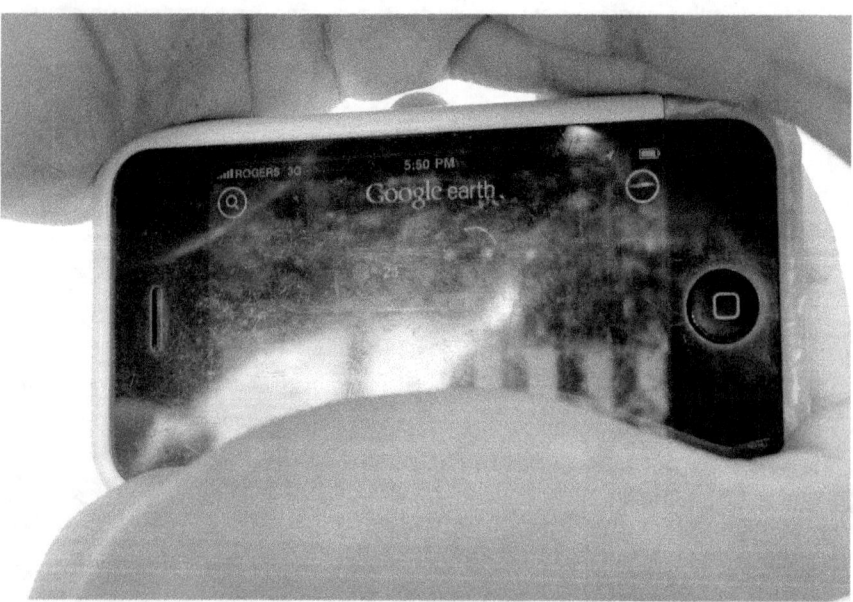

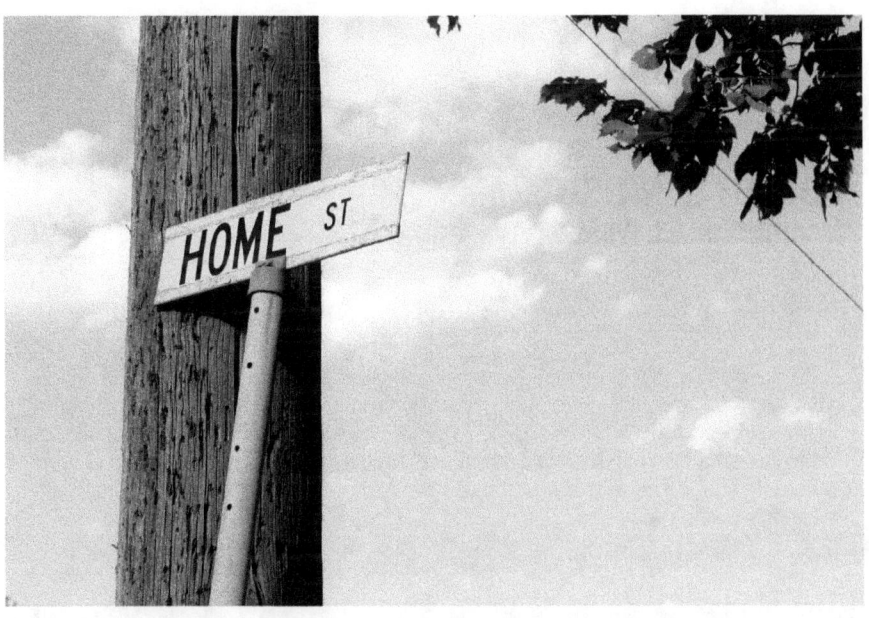

Please choose a dot on the map or a photo on the wall and tell us what you think of it.

Location: Ellice Avenue + Home St.

Liked/Disliked: Liked

Why: Simple, positive, Reminds me of I see Winnipeg as home. Has a Winnipeg feel to it.

Mother's Music
Placemarker 43: Wolever Ave. and Wall St.

"Mother's Music is a division of Gordon Price Music, their Winnipeg location is situated on Wall street. The store sells musical instruments, amps, DJ equipment, anything you need to kick off your band." (Mother's Music) The building sits amongst other industrial and commercial companies. Their sign resembles some sort of retro 60s rocket ship. The security gate has a mural that is only visible after-store hours when it is pulled down.

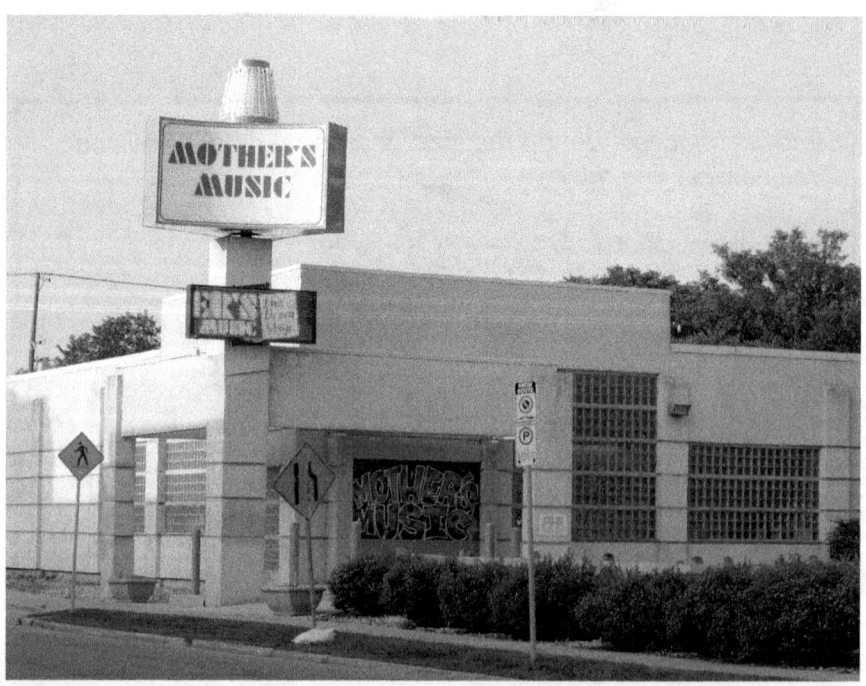

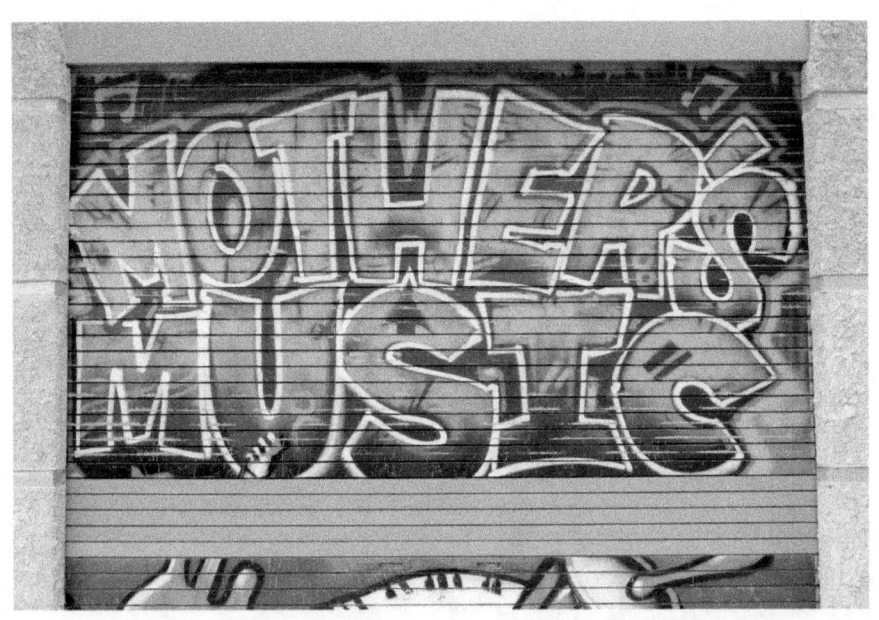

Winnipeg Mural's inform us that the mural was made by Pat Lazo and Fred Thomas and it reads "Mother's Music" with a playful guitar, piano, and drum kit jamming along the bottom of the door. The windows of the shop have multiple cube textured glass to obscure an outsider's vision to mask what lies within the interior. This speciality shop is situated in an odd corner of the West End and isn't exactly discrete.

The West Wall Mural by Anna Scott
Placemarker 64: back alley of Kennedy & Edmonton

Behind a vacant store front within an alleyway near portage place is a brightly coloured mural. With hot air balloons, birds and UFOs floating above a dumpster, in the back exit of the Magic Nail salon one cannot be curious why there is a mural here. There are helicopters, dropping gifts and a smiling monkey climbing a sky-scraper while ice-cream trucks are below him and hearts are floating through the air. "I heart Winnipeg" is marked on one of the air balloons and a joyous crowd of people are depicted running through the streets.

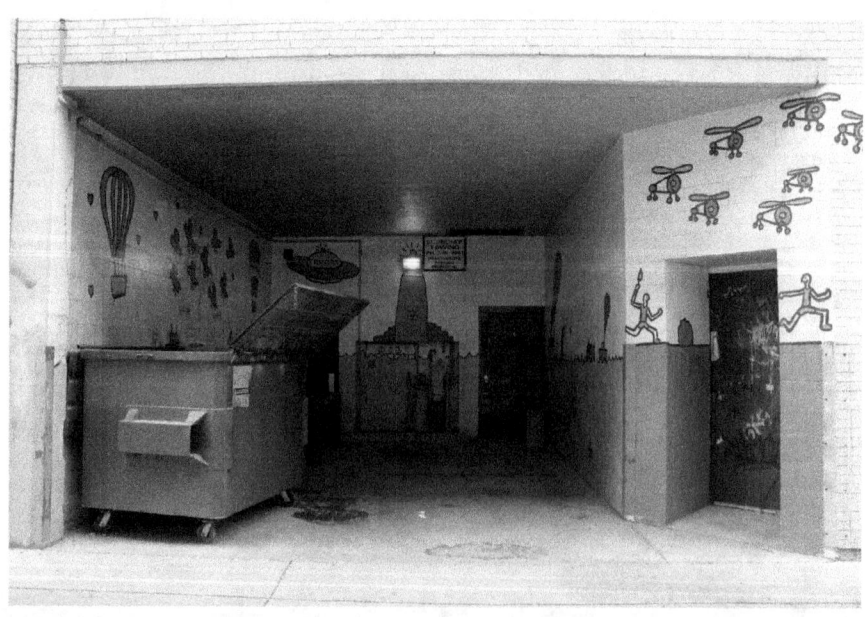

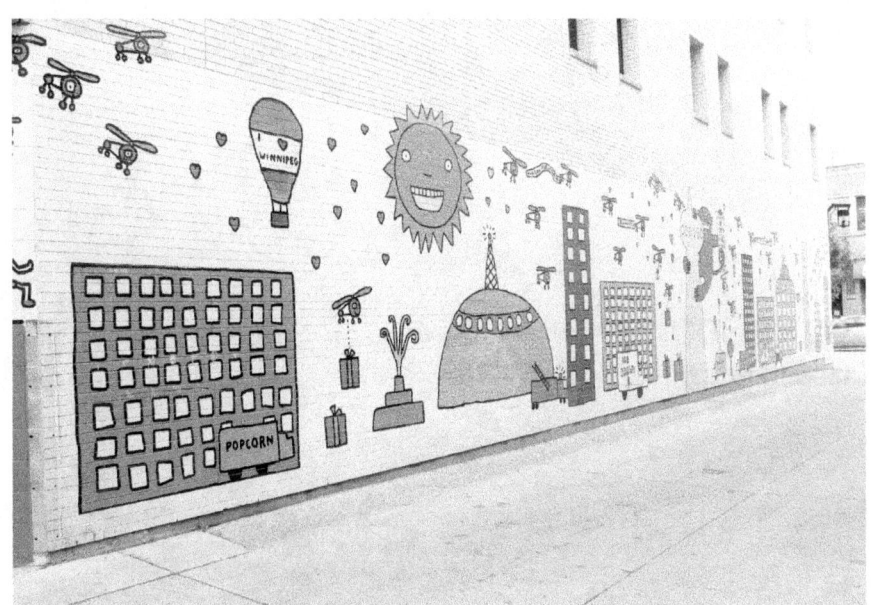

The mural was created by Anna Scott in 1997 and commissioned by "Take Pride Winnipeg" and "D-7 Property. What is currently at the location is a more "upbeat" revision of the original mural. The first images produced by Anna had "All of those helicopters were shooting gas and bullets at the monkey! And all those cars and trucks at the bottom were shooting bullets! And the people on the ground were all Devils! And the monkey had a large banana and he was attacking the helicopters! It was a very simplistic mural but I didn't want violence." - Tom Ethans (Executive Director of Take Pride Winnipeg

The new piece was geared to take a young person's perspective and to display some terrific elements of Winnipeg. Parts of the mural represent the flood in Winnipeg that year, and paid tribute to the Flood Fighters. There is an ice-cream truck with a triple decker ice-cream cone on the side of the vehicle. "This represents my philosophy of life. Each of the ice cream scoops on the cone looks like a sideways 'D': Dedication, Determination and Discipline. You need those in order to succeed. Right? But if you have all those three things you still can fail without the cone, which is an upside down 'A' for Attitude."

The additional information about the site was found on The Murals of Winnipeg website.

Aqua Books
Placemarker 178: 274 Garry St.

Aqua Books, was a favorite spot in Winnipeg. It was self-explanatory as it seemed to be a unique hub of activity that was definitely a distinctive Winnipeg concoction. At the Tallest Poppy we gained some insight from it's owner.

Please choose a dot on the map or a photo on the wall and tell us what you think of it.

Location: 274 GARRY ST

Liked/Disliked: LIKE

Why: I LIKE IT BECAUSE I OWN THE BUILDING. I'M THERE MORE THAN I AM @ HOME. IT'S MY GIFT TO THE CITY

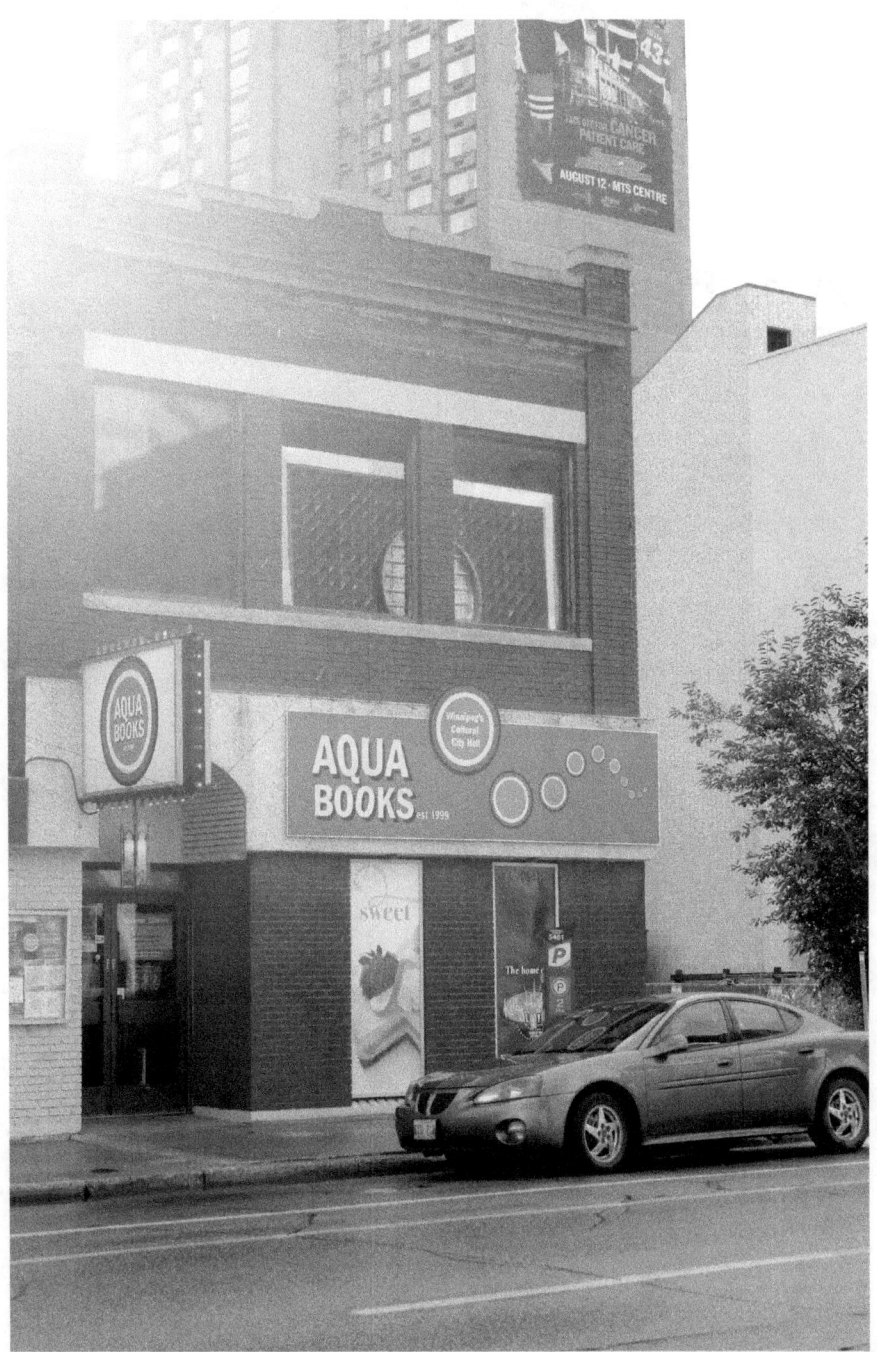

Under the bridge of the Forks
Placemarker 319: East of Main St.

Hidden away from the developed touristy Forks, this is an after-hours hang out. In-dents in the bush hint back to groups creating a path down to the river. Remnants of gatherings lay on the worn ground that is now a hardened rich dirt. It is damp, cool and shady, a prefect summer hiding place from the beating sun.

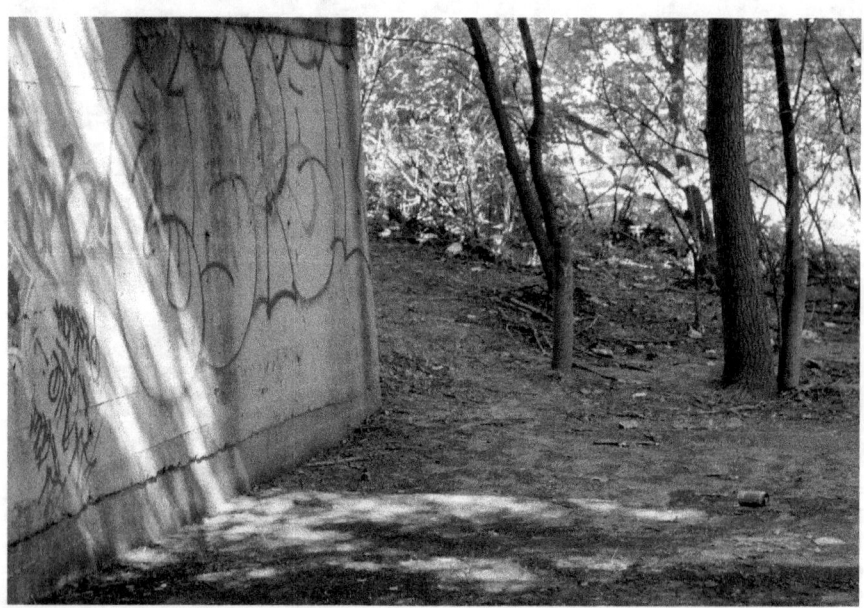

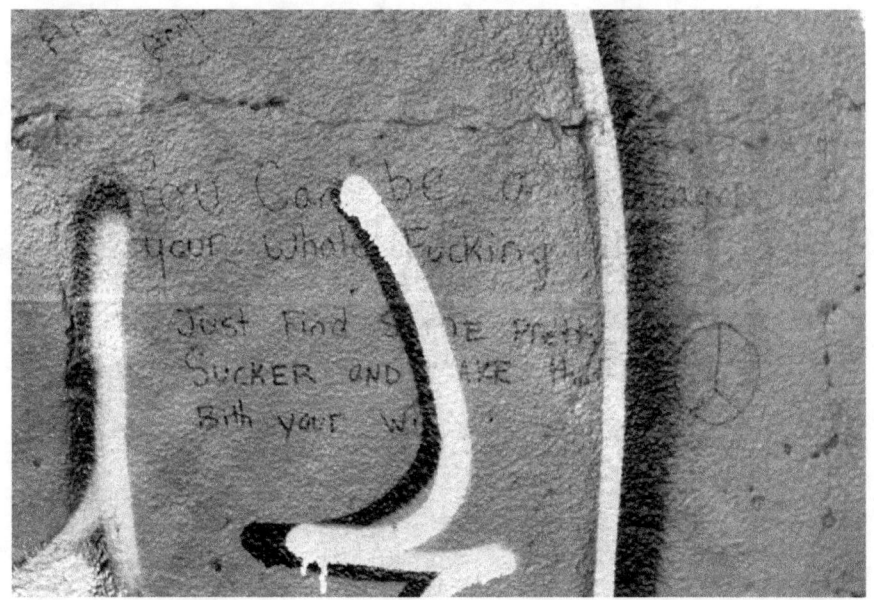

Empty liquor bottles are scattered around, while teenage voices are sharpied on the bridge support. These messages stay here, waiting for the authors to return and continue the passage. They will return when the sun falls toting drinks in their hands, laughter in the air, and secrets to share.

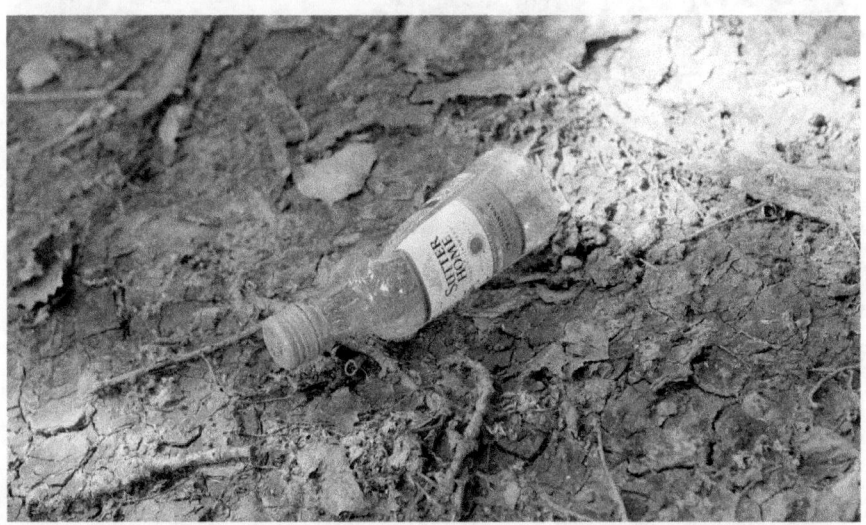

Philly Cheese and Steak Shack
Placemarker 401: Pioneer/Water Ave. and Westbrook St.

With the parking lot bustling and the strumming of Almost Famous in the not so distant background, this place stands alone in silence. It sits on William Stephenson Way formerly know as Water Ave, the street sign rests in its original spot only to be crossed out in black and the new sign placed directly under it. The opposite side of the underpass from Canwest park, you can almost imagine the liveliness that went on in this spot before now.

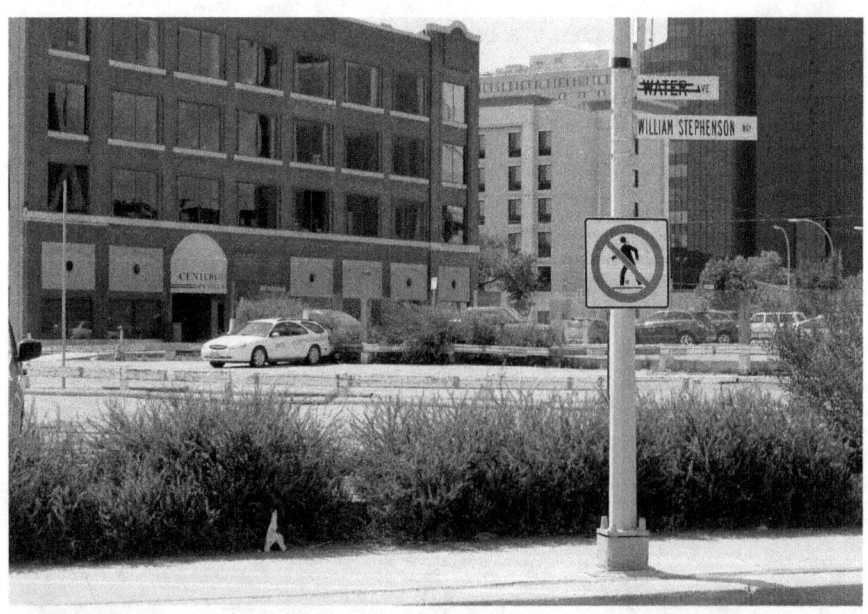

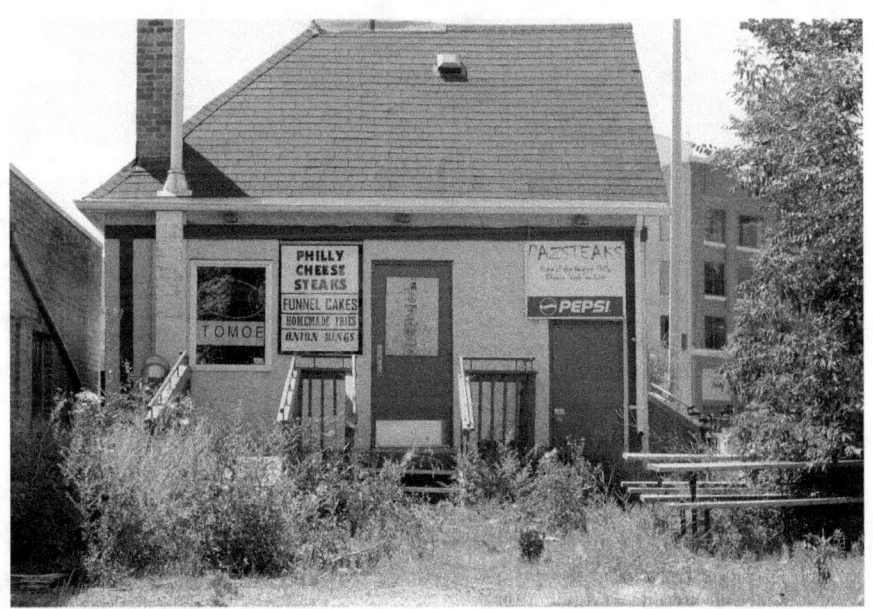

Its game-day and the city is gathering together 10 meters away, this shack will not receive attention from local pedestrians. It sits in ghost like silence, hinting back to a different time. The grass has grown long and has yellowed, it sways in the breeze. Both entrances are boarded up, leaving you to wonder what kind of state the inside is in. A picnic table still sits on the lot. Even now the menu is nailed to the wall promoting the "Pazsteaks Home of the Original Philly Cheese Steak Sandwich."

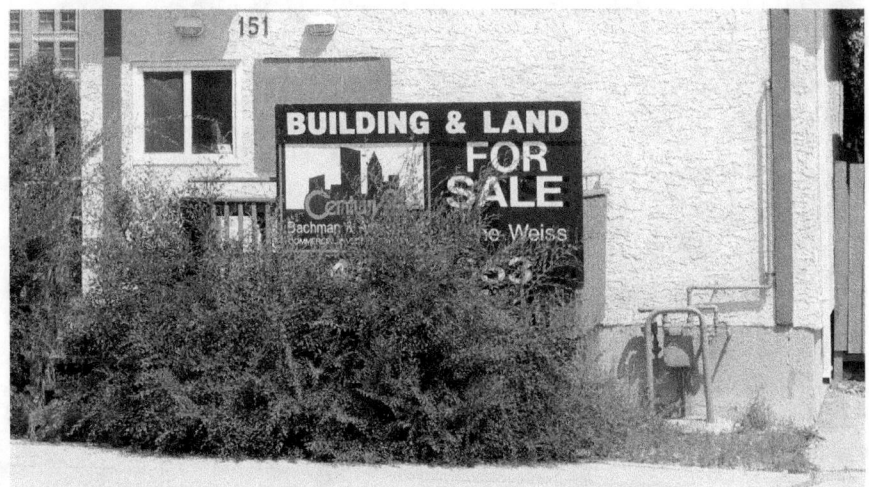

The Banana Boat
Placemarker 401: Osborne St. and Don Ave.

Someone's eyes are lit and delighted by these words on this bulletin board "Happy Birthday Lyle, I love you." followed by another snicker and chuckle on the other side "Congrats Trish and Dennis, the bun is out of the over." These messages are from the customers of the Banana Boat, who have rented the board to make announcements for birthdays, anniversaries, and other special events.

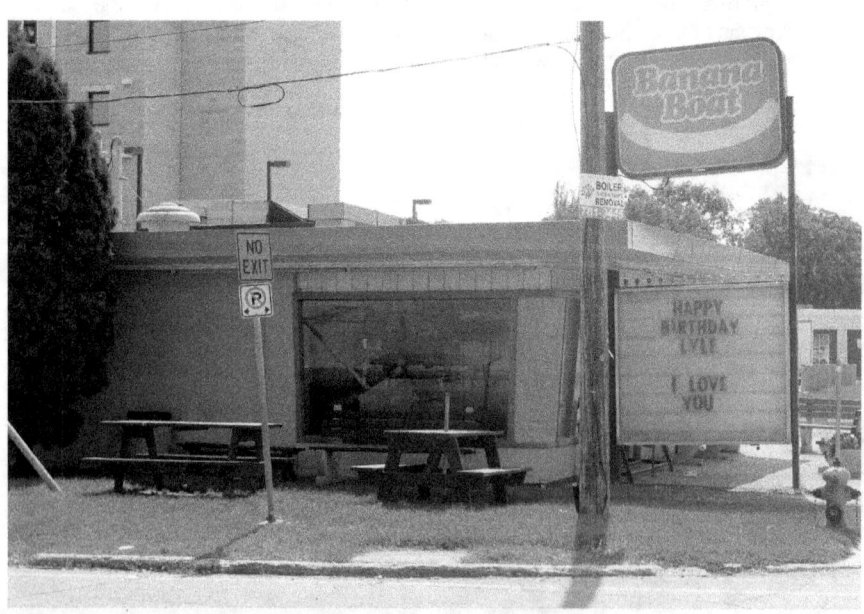

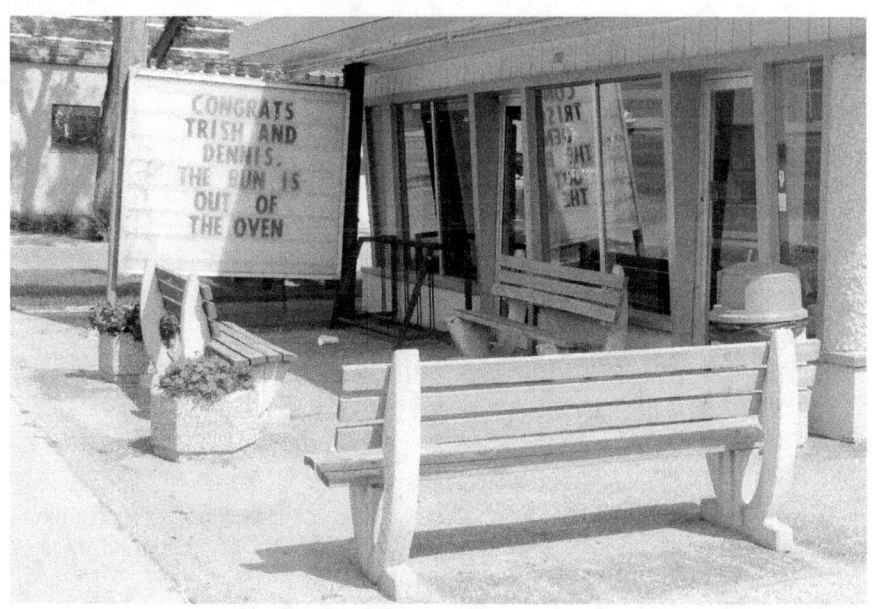

This bright blue and yellow building is an ice-cream pallor that serves your favourite hand and soft served frozen treats. The establishment is located on Osborne and has been opened since 1977. Don Togo Park and it's riverside bike path is behind the pallor and it's terrace with picnic tables and bench.

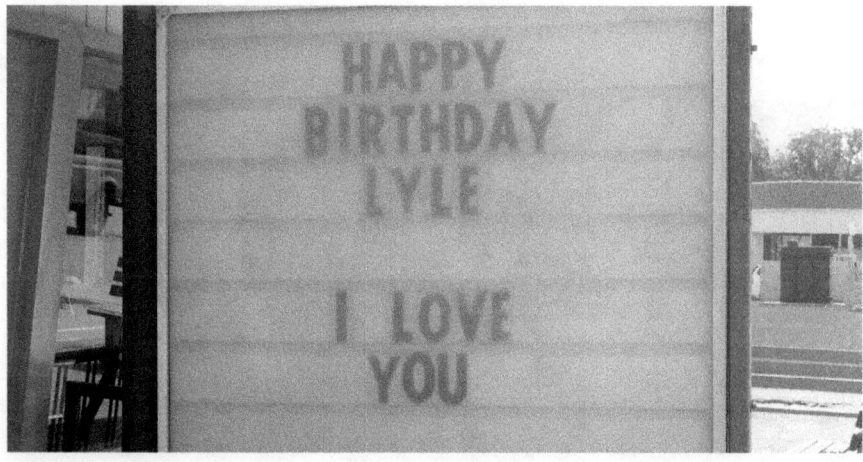

Fort Rouge Bus Terminal
Placemarker 118: Brandon Ave. and Osborne St.

Hidden within the Fort Rouge neighbourhood, this site stands bare amongst the densely forested streets. With a monochromatic ocean of concrete, an individual feels more like an ant stranded on the sidewalk on a hot summer day. Much like a hive or anthill, the terminus is in a constant state of motion. Large city buses looming and out of their cave like garages. The structure is reminiscent of the late 60's early 70's industrial aesthetic. Designed by D.M. Jesson in 1969 the terminus remains, "an example of large scale industrial architecture whose impact relies on scale and silhouette."(Thompson p.25)

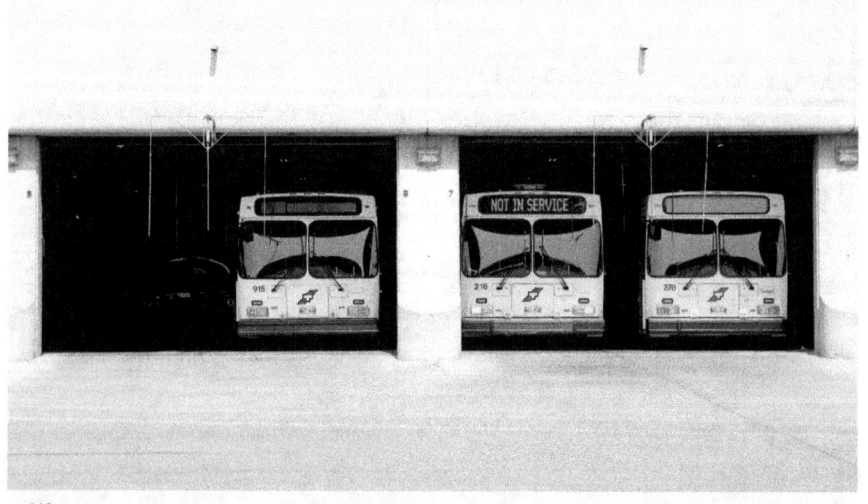

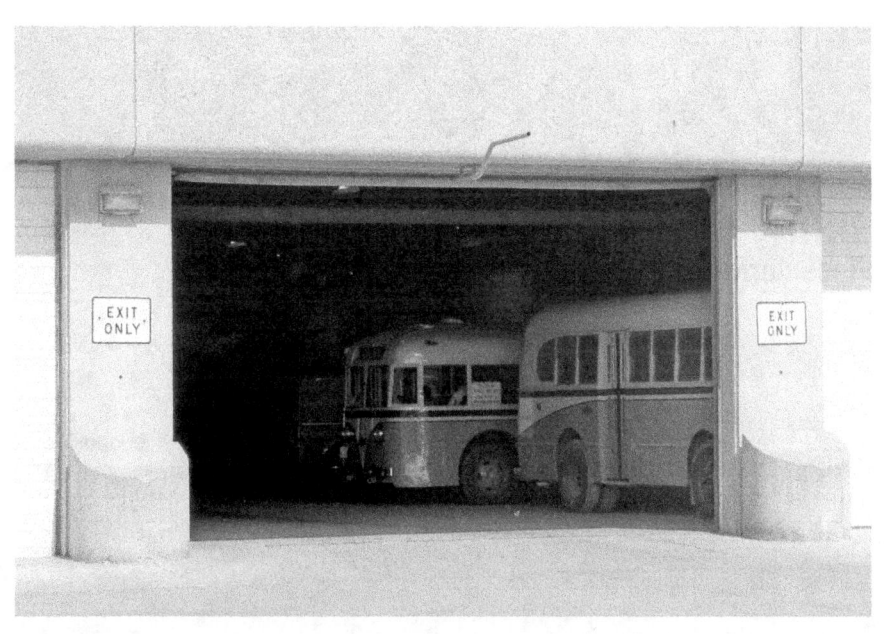

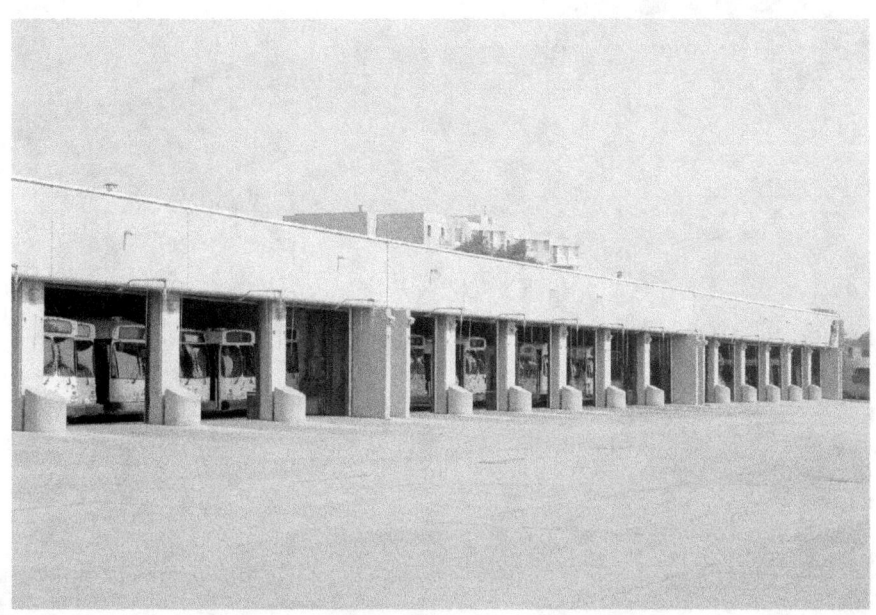

Jenny J's Cookie Bouquets
Placemarker 216: Osborne St. and Hethrington Ave.

Across from St. Mary's Cemetery is a bright lime green bakery named "Jenny J's Cookie Bouquets." With their slogan "For all seasons, For any reason". Her cookies are baked fresh from scratch with no additives, preservatives and are trans fat free. These tasty treats are individually wrapped in cellophane and topped with a bow. Sitting in the window front are several different vehicles ranging from fire trucks, pickup trucks, construction trucks, and locomotives. They are all carrying delicious treats to make this Father's day complete.

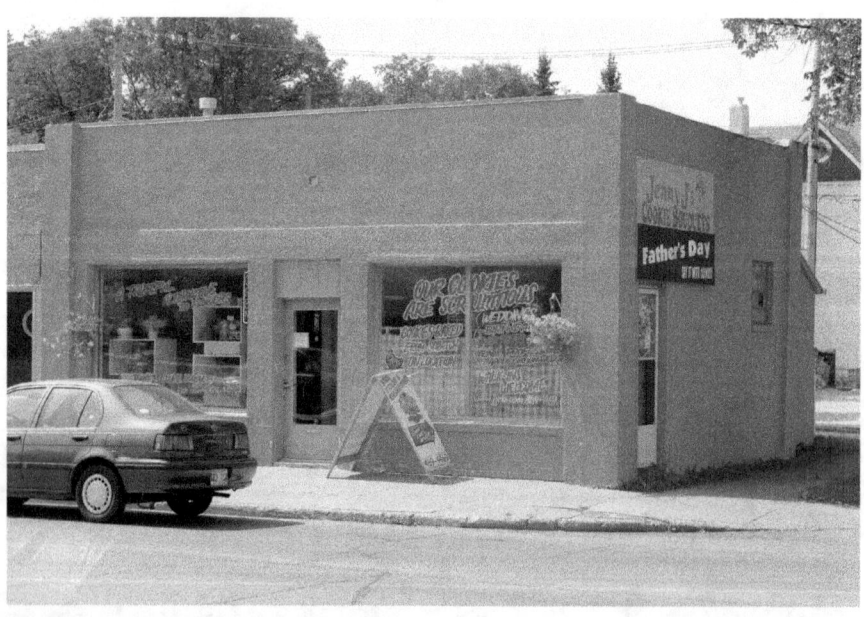

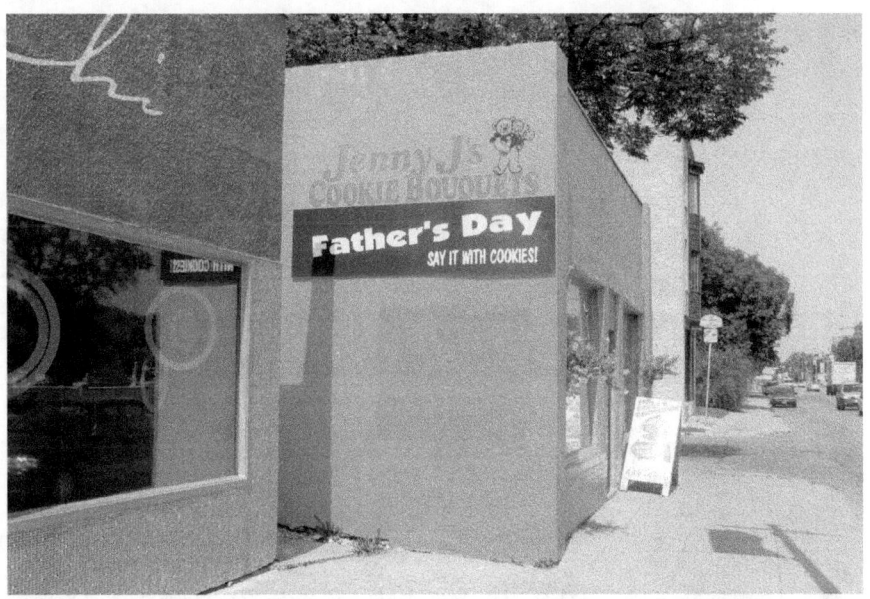

A definite eye catcher to the everyday pedestrian, the building itself seems to resemble that of a common store front. Jenny has definitely taken a bare structure and has added playful text and eccentric colors to the very dull and gray neighbour hood that surrounds the establishment.

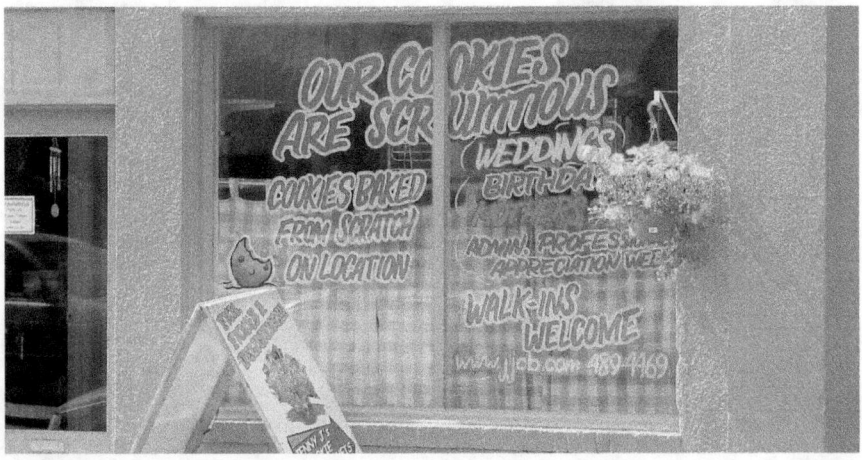

One Willow Tree by a dead end
Placemarker 120: Nassau St. by the Pembina Highway

A short bike down the Pemina highway lead us to this cul-de-sac at the end of several different garage driveways. A tall willow tree sits in the middle of this concrete round about, swaying back and forth. This favoured spot isn't too far from traffic flow, it's waiting for the kids to come home and for misguided directions to circle it. Garage doors and backyard gardens surround the site and our tired eyes pan back and forth waiting for another sound.

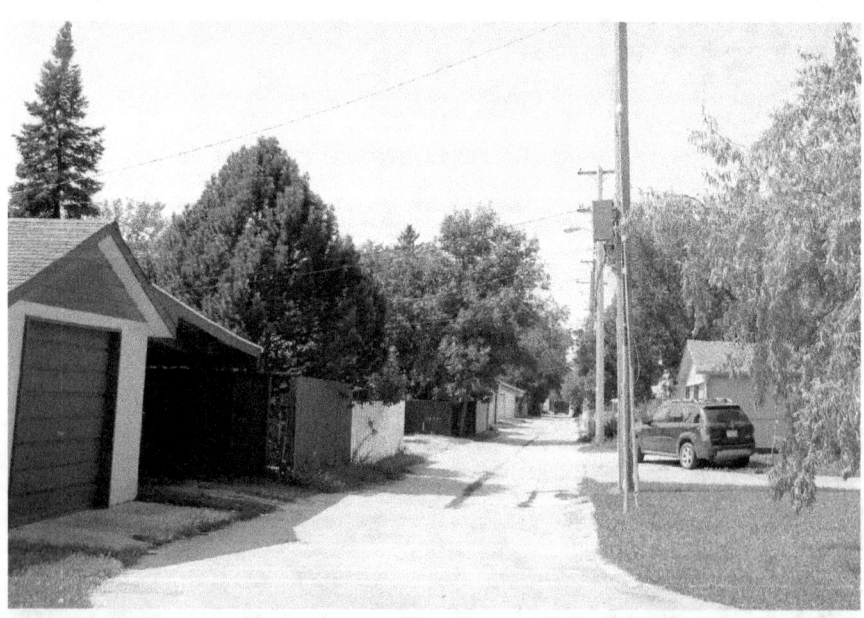

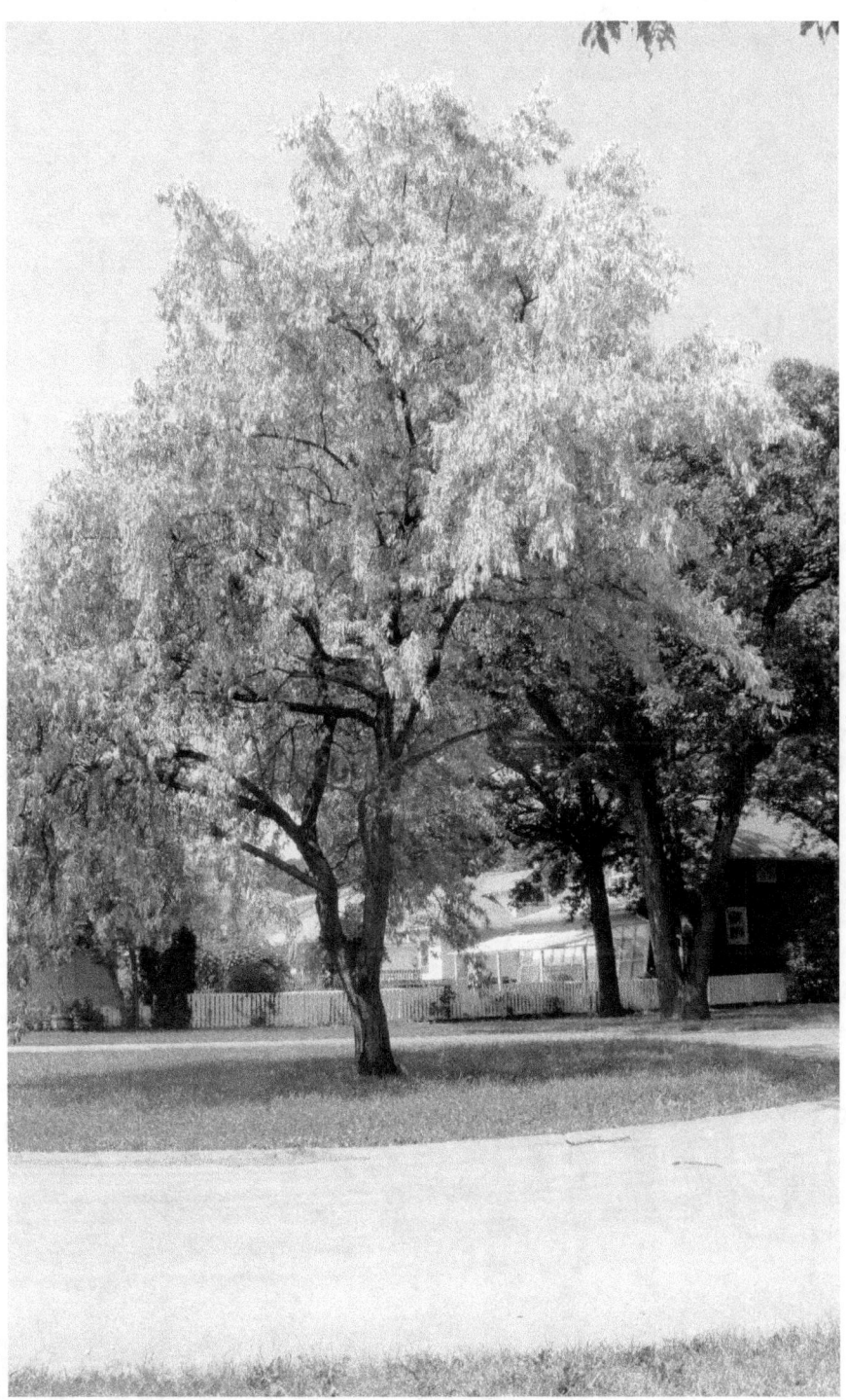

Bob's Transmissions
Placemarker 414: Pembina Highway and Ebby Ave

Located just south from downtown on Pembina is a small garage named "Bob's Transmissions." The establishment first started in 1974, and is currently still open. The building is being repainted, changing it's original black and white color scheme, to a gray tone while persevering it's original logo from the 70s.

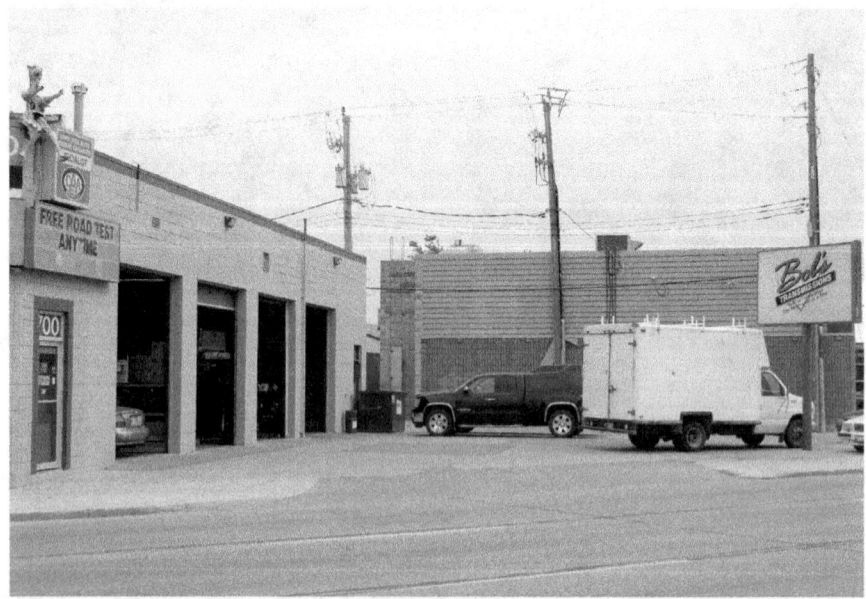

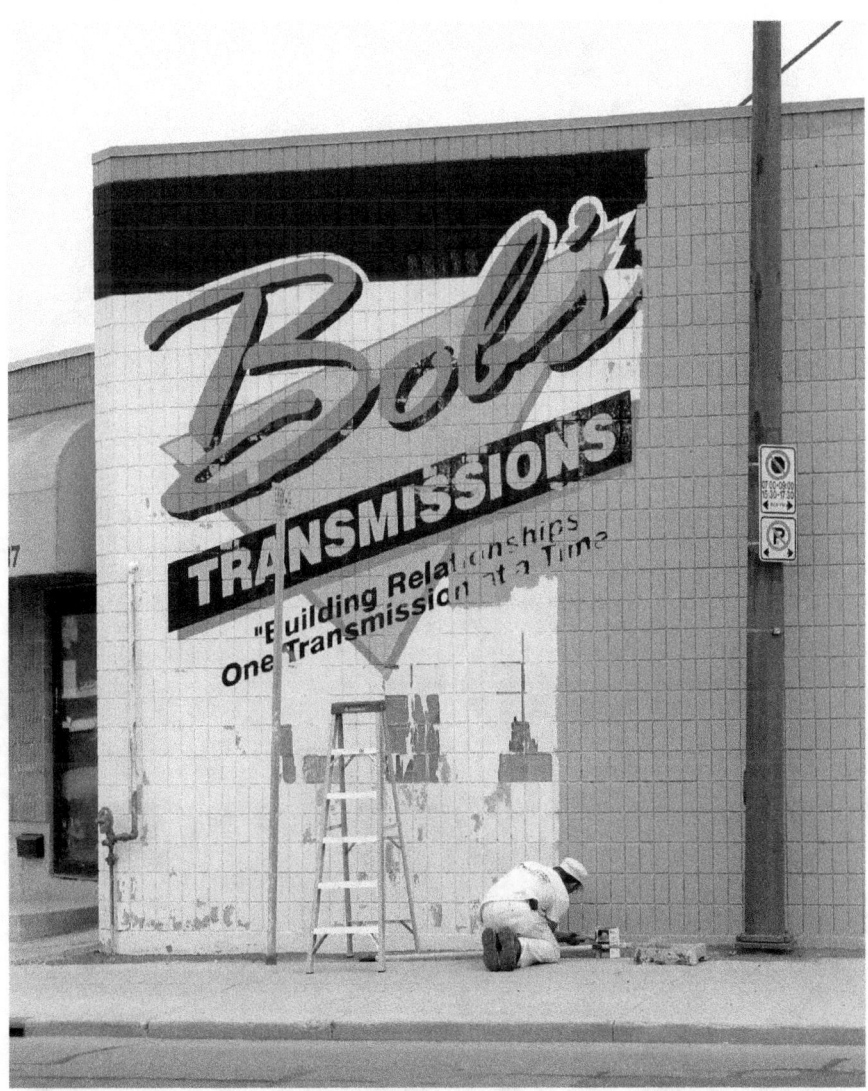

Their slogan is "Building relationships one transmission at a time." Sitting on top of the shop is a sculpture resembling some type of robot-like figure built from used car parts. It becomes clear that local shops and small auto garage within the area embrace their customer's loyalty.

Garage with Kittens
Placemarker 82: Austin Ave and Logan St

At this North Point Douglas garage, one car sits on the exterior of the parking lot. The car is abandoned and wrecked beyond repair. The hood is removed, leaving the engine bear from the elements, indents cover the body, and no wheels remain. Rust is devouring the original "Winnipeg black" Pontiac paint job. With a little research and help from the Manitoba Pontiac Association, this car turned out to be a 1962 Pontiac Parisienne. This car would have been built in Oshawa Canada, and shipped to a Pontiac dealership in the area, like Winnipeg Motor Products.

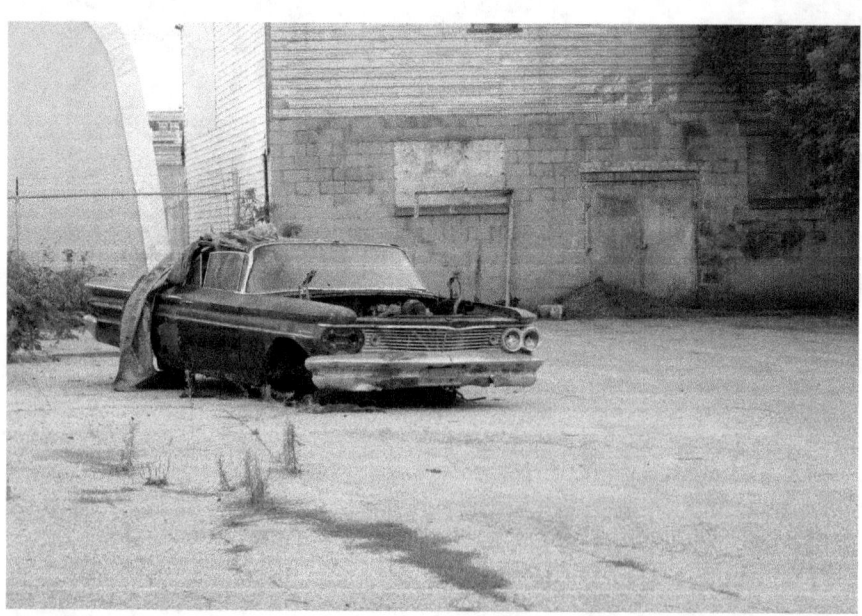

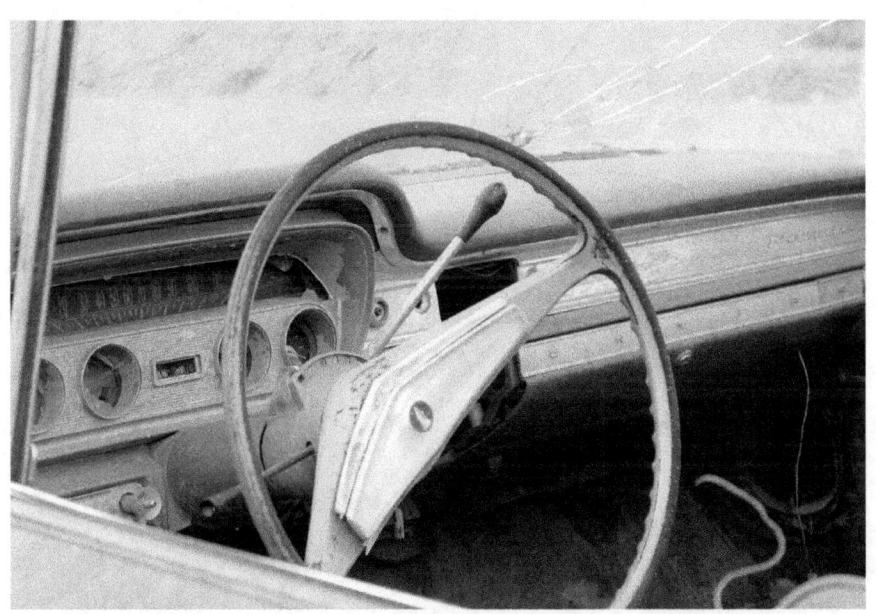

An air of spontaneity and a sense of tenderness came about when the car's new purpose was revealed. The interior of the car had become a safe haven for a mother cat and her three kittens. Someone had thrown a tarp over the car to keep them dry in the rain, and left canned soft food underneath the car's trunk on the asphalt. It was a heartfelt surprise seeing the work of a strangers kindness.

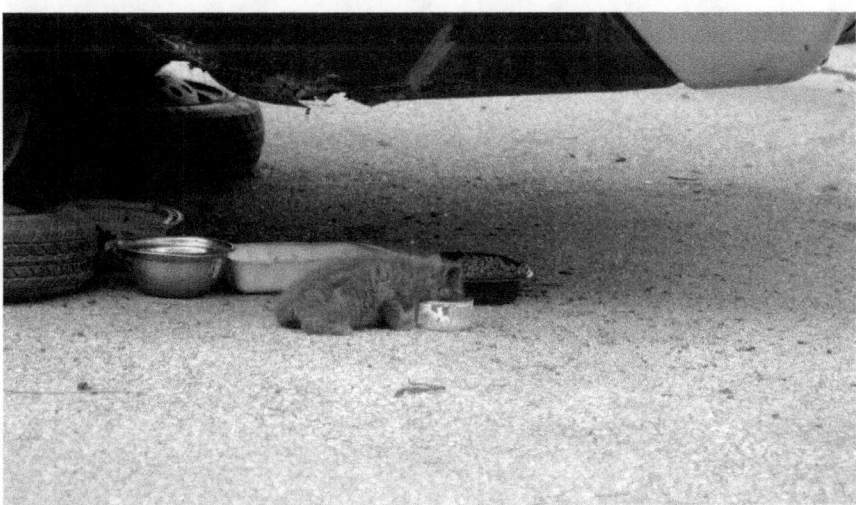

Bibliography

Banana Boat, Web Sept 4, 2010.

Bertrand, Bob, Our Service, Testimonials, on *Bob's Transmissions-- Transmission Repair-Winnipeg, Manitoba-Canada,* Web Sept 20, 2010.

Hunka, Jeremy, Opening of new airport terminal delayed until 2011, in *CTV Winnipeg,* Web Sept 23, 2010.

Keshavjee, Serena, *Winnipeg modern : architecture, 1945-1975,* Winnipeg : University of Manitoba Press, 2006.

Jenny J's Cookie Bouquets, Web 2008.

The Murals of Winnipeg, Web Oct 8, 2010.

Thompson, William Paul. *Winnipeg Architecture: 100 years,* Winnipeg; Queenston House, 1975.

Von Stackelberg, Katia, Welcome to the Corydon Avenue BIZ, in *Welcome to Corydon Avenue,* Web Aug 30, 2010.

Welcome to the online home of Mother's Music...Your Canadian Music Store serving Western Canada!, on *Mother's Music,* Web Sept 15, 2010.

Portage and Main, on *Wikipedia.* Web Sept 19, 2010.